The Struggle for Human and Economic Development in Sub-Saharan Africa

THE STRUGGLE FOR HUMAN AND ECONOMIC DEVELOPMENT IN SUB-SAHARAN AFRICA

By

BRUCE A. FORSTER
and
JESSICA D. FORSTER

With
KELLI E. FORSTER

NorthAmerican
Business Press
Atlanta – Seattle – South Florida – Toronto

North American Business Press, Inc
Atlanta, Georgia
Seattle, Washington
South Florida
Toronto, Canada

Struggles for Development in Sub-Saharan Africa: The Good, the Bad and the Ugly
ISBN: 9780985394905

Along with trade books for various business disciplines, the North American Business Press also publishes a variety of academic-peer reviewed journals.

Library of Congress Control Number: 2012951021

Library of Congress
Cataloging in Publication Division
101 Independence Ave., SE
Washington, DC 20540-4320
Printed in theUnited States of America

First Edition

DEDICATION

The authors dedicate the book to the following family members:

Jeremy and Hilary Forster

and

Trevor, Mataya and Summer Spaidal

ACKNOWLEDGEMENTS

Ironically, the work on this book was enabled by a sudden health problem which resulted in my early retirement. My ability to keep working on this topic, which became this book, is due to the fantastic medical teams who provided excellent care. Accordingly, I thank Drs. Vosik and Islam as the primary members in Kearney, and Drs. Sorrell and Miles with the organ transplant unit of the University of Nebraska Medical Center in Omaha.

Darci Kuhnel, owner of the Breakfast Cart in Kearney, was kind enough to allow me to escape cabin fever and to spend a few hours each morning using her internet access. She and her staff kept me fueled with coffee and the best omelets I have ever had.

The authors thank the personnel at NABP. We appreciated the receptiveness of Dr. Jeffrey Kennedy and Dr. Adam Davidson to the initial idea for the book. Thanks go to Marius Lazau for overseeing the editorial aspects of the manuscript once it was submitted.

For the development of the maps of Africa we thank Professor John Bauer of the University of Nebraska at Kearney.

Finally, we thank the members of our family for their support and encouragement. Specifically we thank:

> Son and brother, Jeremy Forster and his wife Hilary Forster
> and
> Kelli's husband Trevor Spaidal and their daughters Mataya and Summer Spaidal

ABOUT THE AUTHORS

Dr. Bruce A. Forster holds a BA in Mathematics and Economics from the University of Guelph in Canada, and a Ph.D. in Economics from the Australian National University. He is co-author of Economics in Canadian Society (John Wiley), and author of The Acid Rain Debate: Science and Special Interests in Policy Formation (Iowa State University). He has also written almost 50 journal articles, book chapters and special proceedings. From 1989 to 1991, Dr. Forster was an Associate Editor of the Journal of Environmental Economics and Management. He served as an environmental consultant to government agencies in Canada and the US Environmental Agency. Dr. Forster taught a course on International Trade and Finance each summer from 1990 to 2002 for the Taiwan government's Academy of International Economic Affairs. From 1991 to 2009, Dr. Forster served as a Business dean at the University of Wyoming, Arizona State University's West campus, and the University of Nebraska at Kearney. Bruce is currently John Becker Endowed Professor, Emeritus and Professor of Economics, Emeritus at UNK. He is also Professor, Emeritus at ASU.

Jessica D. Forster holds a BA in Political Science and Latin American Studies, with a Spanish Minor, from the University of Arizona, and an LLM in International Law with International Relations from the University of Kent's Brussels School of International Studies. While working on her Masters studies, Jessica spent three weeks as a volunteer in Kenya. After completing her dissertation on violence to women and child refugees in Africa she was employed by the Somali Bantu Association of Tucson, Arizona which is devoted to assisting recent refugees from Africa. She also worked with the Somali Bantu Association of Nebraska. Jessica continues to work with refugees and immigrant communities in Toronto, Canada. Jess is also pursuing a Master's degree in Adult Education and Community Development at the University of Toronto.

Kelli E. Forster holds a BA in Psychology from the University of British Columbia. Following graduation Kelli travelled in Ghana and Burkina Faso. She has also travelled in South-east Asia. From 1997-2005, Kelli worked for Creo Inc. in Vancouver, BC, Canada. From 2005-2012 worked for Schneider Electric (formerly Xantrex). Kelli is currently Director of Human Resources at Endurance Wind Power.

FORWARD

About five years ago, after I had finished giving my standard lecture on "Trends in the World Economy," a student approached me and complimented me on the lecture for the number of regions of the world covered. He then asked why I made no reference to Africa. I was caught off-guard but offered a quick, and totally inadequate, response. Of course, the student was an African. I decided to gain some understanding of what was happening in Africa. Little did I realize that this would be a long-term undertaking. Shortly after starting to write seriously, I realized that my daughter Jessica's Master's thesis was on international humanitarian law applied to violence to women and children in refugee camps in Africa and the Middle East. Her work dove-tailed with a paper I was writing on governance and civil war. We turned the paper into a joint paper and followed it up with more work. Later my daughter Kelli talked to me about the psychological aspects that I hadn't considered, and another avenue of study opened up. This book is the result of my own endeavors and combined efforts with Jessica and Kelli. To work with my daughters has been a very special experience. The final result is much richer than it would have been without their insights and contributions.

CONTENTS

CHAPTER 1
INTRODUCTION

THE "OBJECT" OF STUDY

In this book we survey issues impacting the economic and human development of Sub-Saharan Africa (SSA). SSA makes up a substantial portion of the continent of Africa. Africa, which covers almost 12 million square miles of territory (22% of the earth's total landmass), is the second largest of the earth's seven continents. Africa is believed to be the region where the human race evolved, and subsequent outmigration(s) populated the other regions of the world.

North Africa and Sub-Saharan Africa (SSA)

Africa naturally divides into two major portions: North Africa and Sub-Saharan Africa (SSA). The Sahara Desert serves as a natural divide between the countries of North Africa and Sub-Saharan Africa (SSA) with North Africa lying to the north of, and including large portions of the Sahara, and generally bordering the Mediterranean Sea (Western Sahara is on the Atlantic coast). The specific countries included in North Africa are: Western Sahara, Morocco, Tunisia, Libya, and Egypt. The people of North African countries are predominantly Arab and Muslim.

SSA lies predominantly to the south of the Sahara, and consists of all other African countries and territories not encompassed by North Africa. While this demarcation is straight-forward and will serve our purpose, there are variants found in other research that remove them from the SSA list. These will be acknowledged in a later discussion found in Chapter 3.

Objectives

This book is intended to introduce the reader to the concepts, and statistical measures, involved in the study of human and economic development in SSA. We introduce the reader to notions of state governance, state failure, civil war and various health matters. We consider the profiles of displaced persons and the challenges they face. We consider the development of international laws, and the violations of these laws and the impacts of such violations. Sub-Saharan Africa serves both as the central subject of our study and as a guide for similar studies of other developing regions of the world. Many of the Tables included provide statistical comparisons for the other developing regions of the world. Where statistical measures of other regions are not provided, the

"Source" material will generally direct the reader to appropriate reference material.

AUDIENCE

We expect that our book will appeal to two distinct audiences. One is individuals who seek to learn more about what is occurring in Sub-Saharan Africa. The other audience includes professors and students of courses about Africa or related topics. For example, relevant courses include courses in economic development or development economics, international studies with regional emphases that include Africa, world geography with topics in Africa, history of Africa, international political science courses, and any discipline or course focusing on developing countries and regions of the world.

The Importance of this Book and Its Topics

The *2009 Global Monitoring Report* noted that the countries making the most sluggish progress towards meeting the Millennium Development Goals (see below) are those fragile and conflict-affected states. More than half of these countries are in Sub- Saharan Africa (SSA). Collier (2007), in the book *The Bottom Billion*, comments that 73% of those people living in the bottom billion of people globally have been through a civil war or are still engaged in one. Many of these wars occur in SSA. Collier refers to civil war as [economic] development in reverse. In discussing the costs of war, Collier points out that many who die as a result of civil war are not combatants killed in active combat but rather civilian, non-combatants who succumb to disease. The wars generate mass migrations of involuntarily displaced persons and collapsing public health systems which create epidemics. As displaced persons, women and children are particularly vulnerable to risks. A body of international law has evolved to protect such displaced persons and non-combatants in general. Unfortunately, these laws frequently are ignored, and as a result many people suffer. Many die from disease as noted, but others die from starvation. The suffering is not only through premature death and may last for prolonged periods of time. The deep scars received early on from experiencing horrific events, directly or through observation, can fester in individuals over time mentally and emotionally. People are beginning to consider the long-term impacts of Post-Traumatic Stress Disorder for Africa's displaced persons.

The United Nations (UN) Millennium Declaration

In a strong showing of support for strengthening economic and human development in Developing Countries, 189 countries signed the United Nations Millennium Declaration at the UN's Millennium Summit in September 2000. Central to the Declaration is the specification of a set of eight Millennium Development Goals (MDGs) The MDGs echo earlier goals embodied in the results of other meetings such as the 1991 World Health Conference on Population and Development (the Cairo Consensus), the 1996 World Food Summit, and the 2000 World Education Forum. The MDGs provide the official framework for supporting and assessing human and economic development. The set of MDGs also provides a useful vehicle for discussing development issues facing individual Developing Countries as well as regions of the world. The spirit of the MDGs was reaffirmed by the 2005 UN World Summit. Support for the Declaration has been affirmed at the G8 Gleneagles Summit in Gleneagles, Scotland, by the G20 London (UK) Summit, and by the 2010 UN World Summit.

We examine SSA's performance on the set of MDGs relative to other regions of the world. We also consider various indicators not captured by the usual treatments of the MDGs, and discuss issues more broadly where it seems reasonable to do so.

Approach/Methodology of the Book

Our approach focuses on "secondary source" research. We synthesize substantial amounts of works, some of which frequently is not published in academic journals. Many studies are in publications of special international groups such as UNICEF, USAID, UNAIDS, World Wild-Life Fund and so forth. The reader will be introduced to the variety of sources as he/she proceeds since this is one of the learning objectives as well.

OUTLINE OF THE BOOK'S COVERAGE

Chapters 2-4 set the background for the study of Africa and SSA in particular. Chapter 2 provides a "reader's digest" version of the history of Africa starting with Africa as the source of the origin of the human species and coming up in large steps to modern times including the colonial and independence periods. Africa is a land of many contrasts. In Chapter 2 we look at some of the contrasts under the headings: the Good, the Bad and the Ugly (apologies to the movie). Chapter 3 considers various classifications of countries in SSA. Some are based upon economic features. This Chapter considers the countries which are designated as Least Developed Countries and those designated as Heavily Indebted Poor Countries. Some countries are classified by geographic characteristics such as those which are land-locked versus those that are coastal. Another category is the set of small island developing countries. Chapter 3 also considers the political systems in various countries. Chapter 4 considers population and economic growth. A very brief overview of population growth over history is given. Basically it took all of human time until about 1800 for the human population world-wide to grow to 1 billion people. It took only 130 years to reach 2 billion and 30 more years to reach 3 billion in 1960. In the autumn of 2011, the world's population reached 7 billion people! Not only has the world's population grown dramatically, the population density and growth has shifted from developed to developing countries since the middle of the 1900s. Chapter 4 also considers relative economic performance over time. SSA has shown considerable improvement overall in the last decade. Not all SSA countries have shared in this improvement however. Some of the world's poorest countries are in SSA as noted in Chapter 3.

Chapter 5 introduces the student to the concept of state governance (as opposed to corporate governance which has received a lot of attention in the last several years). The definition and measures of good governance are considered. The consequences of poor governance include state failure and possibly civil conflict. The chapter introduces the reader to concepts and measures of state failure. Corruption and the Corruption Perception Index are introduced. The poverty trap as an alternative explanation to poor governance is briefly discussed.

Chapter 5 also introduces the reader to the various definitions of civil strife from civil conflict to armed conflict and to civil war. The causes of civil war are discussed.

Chapter 6 considers the impact that civil conflict has on people. Specifically, the chapter discusses displaced persons noting the distinction between internally displaced persons and refugees along with detailed profiles of these groups in terms of their home countries and, for refugees, their new host countries. The subsequent movements of these groups in returning to their homes or not, and the age/gender composition of displaced persons is discussed. A separate group is Stateless persons who are discussed briefly.

Chapters 7-9 deal with the evolution of international laws, their subsequent violation, and the plausible motives for the violations. We note the distinction between treaty law and customary law, and the relationship between International Human Rights Law and International Humanitarian Law.

In Chapter 7 we deal with international laws that have evolved to protect civilians in times of war. These include the four Geneva Conventions, conventions dealing with genocide and with torture. There are additional bodies of laws to protect women and children and displaced persons. Chapter 7 also outlines the judicial processes and authorities involved in dealing with these laws. Of particular interest are Truth Commissions, International Criminal Tribunals, and a more recent innovation the International Criminal Court.

Codify laws, and you can expect them to be violated. Chapter 8 considers violations of the laws discussed in Chapter 7. Rwanda and Darfur are recent examples of genocide, or at least alleged genocide in the case of Darfur. The President of Sudan is still at large ignoring arrest warrants, one of which is for alleged genocide.

There are many violations of laws protecting women and children. We have chosen one example for each. For women we focus on sexual crimes including rape, and for children we focus on their use as soldiers.

We consider the challenges faced by displaced persons. Refugees and internally displaced persons share some of the same challenges, but each also has separate challenges. Finally, the chapter considers the emotional and psychological damage inflicted by the trials of dealing with war. Experiences in Sudan and the Democratic Republic of Congo serve as examples.

Chapter 9 offers plausible explanations for people violating these laws. Special interests play a strong role in policy formation or obstruction. The actions may be to protect “resources” from being given up or to have them transferred to the offender. Natural resources provide a good example of such resources to seek. The financial proceeds from ownership of such resources may contribute to civil strife and also enable it to continue. The concept of State Sovereignty has allowed dictators to behave badly without the threat of outside intervention since they proclaim their sovereignty.

Chapters 10-12 discuss the performance of SSA and other developing regions on the Millennium Development Goals (MDGs). Chapter 10 addresses the first three MGDs: Poverty and Hunger, Education and Gender Equity. In addition to the poverty measures specified for the poverty goal, we introduce the reader to some alternative measures. These include the Human Development Index (HDI) and the Inequality-adjusted HDI. Similarly with hunger, we expand the treatment to include concepts of protracted food crises, as defined by the FAO, and the Global Hunger Index.

For education we consider the proportions of school age children enrolled in school. We also discuss the factors impacting the quality of education. We discuss measures of literacy as measures of educational success

For gender equity, measures of equity are presented, and a new measure, the Gender Inequality Index is introduced.

Chapter 11 covers MGDs IV-VI which examine health-related goals: Child, Infant and Maternal Mortality, HIV/AIDS, Malaria and Other Diseases. The standard statistics for child, infant and maternal mortality in SSA and other regions are presented. Similar coverage is given to HIV/AIDS, malaria, tuberculosis, and measles.

Chapter 12 deals with just one MDG: Environmental Sustainability. This is a very large Goal. We examine just a few targets: global climate change, water quality and urban slums. We do not engage in the full debate concerning the greenhouse effect. We examine one impact associated with the warming that has contributed to famine conditions in east Africa, the Horn of Africa. It has been most severe in Somalia. We discuss the methodology for assessing the presence of famine.

Water quality concerns the availability of improved drinking water facilities and improved water sanitation facilities. Concern with urban slums considers the proportion of urban populations living in slum conditions in SSA.

Chapter 13 provides an introduction to a relatively new concept: the Responsibility to Protect (R2P). R2P stands as a challenger to the long-standing philosophy of state sovereignty. R2P advocates international intervention in so-called sovereign states when those states seem incapable of protecting their citizens or are persecuting them, and when the offending countries threaten international peace and stability. We consider the use of UN Peacekeeping forces over the last 60 plus years. If the international community is going to intervene militarily in a foreign country's affairs, the important question becomes - who should perform the intervention? We briefly discuss the questions need to be addressed for the best intervention.

Chapter 14 is the final chapter. We do not attempt to take a stand with recommendations since this book has been intended as an overview of issues. We do two things. First we provide a quick addendum to include events unfolding as the manuscript was about to be forwarded to the publisher.

Second, a short set of topics for future consideration is presented. Each of these has an international aspect impacting or involving SSA: human trafficking, maritime piracy, and animal poaching.

CHAPTER 2
OUT OF AFRICA

There is always something new coming out of Africa

> --Anonymous Greek proverb, cited in Feinberg and Solodow (2002)

The above quote, or a version of it, frequently appears in reference works on Africa. One well-known, and perhaps the shortest expression, is *Out of Africa*, which is the title of the 1985 multiple Oscar award-winning film starring Robert Redford and Meryl Streep. The exact origin of the quote is unknown; however, it is presumed to be ancient Greek. The earliest written account is attributed to Aristotle writing in the second or the third quarter of the fourth century B.C. (Aristotle's death occurred in 322). Subsequent written references include those attributed to Pliny (in Latin), and Rabelais (in French). Feinberg and Solodow (2002) suggested that Erasmus influenced the form of the proverb by accidently rewording Pliny's Latin version.

In ancient Greece, the phrase "something new" referred to strange hybrid animals and hence carried a negative connotation, while in today's usage it carries a positive connotation (Feinberg and Solodow, 2002). This mix in itself is like a metaphor for Africa. It can be a bad or good situation depending upon the time and circumstances.

A VERY BRIEF (AND SELECTIVE) HISTORY OF AFRICA

Africa and the Origins of the Human Species

So far the evidence that we have in the world points to Africa as the Cradle of Humankind

> --George Abungu, Director-General of the National Museums of Kenya, cited in BBC (Undated I).

The oldest fossils of the human species' ancestors have been found in Africa (BBC, Undated I). Africa, given that fossil evidence, is believed to be the origin of "human" and "human-like" creatures with humans originating about 1.5 million years ago, and human-like beings originating more like 4.0 million years or more ago. For the first half of the 20th century, the Cradle of Humankind was believed to be in South

Africa since it had the best evidence of human evolution during that time period. The discoveries by the Leaky family in Tanzania and Kenya in the late 1950s and the later discovery of the Lucy remains in Ethiopia caused thinking to shift the Cradle and have it located in East Africa. Research in the last several years is suggesting a return of the Cradle to Southern Africa. Lee Berger of the University of Witwatersrand and his colleagues discovered fossil remains they believe to be an intermediate form between the primitive *Australopithecus* and the Homo genus (Fischman, 2011). Henn et al. (2011) came to a similar conclusion regarding Southern Africa as the origin for modern humans. Their work was based upon DNA analysis. Henn et al. found that Africa's hunter-gatherers exhibit the highest levels of genetic diversity in the world.

With Africa as the "Cradle of Humankind," humans must have migrated from Africa to other parts of the world. The conventional theory is that the outward migration from Africa occurred as a single diaspora which occurred between 60,000 and 70,000 years ago (Naik, 2011). A recent study has suggested an alternative theory in which there was more than a single out-migration from Africa. According the Willerslev et al. (2011) study there were at least two distinct out-migrations from Africa. The first dispersal took the Africans to Australia about 62,000 and 75,000 years ago. The result was the Australian Aborigines which would be one of the oldest continuous populations outside of Africa. A second migration, in this new theory, would have taken place between 25,000 and 38,000 years ago and given rise to Europeans and Asians. This new theory is an interesting and provocative one. Of course, the jury is still out on this new view. More studies will be needed to sort out which view is the more sound explanation of how the world population was distributed.

Africa: 1800 -1914

Europeans, in the early 19th century, began seeking new lands to provide their industries with raw materials and to provide new markets for their products. This outward expansion, or "imperialism," was further spurred on by European national fervor, or "nationalism." In the early part of the century European involvement in Africa was limited to coastal areas. In the middle of the century the Europeans' interest in Africa, as a source of natural resources/raw materials to supply its industrial production at home, grew. In the 1880s, discoveries of gold and diamonds set off a European "scramble for Africa." In 1884-85, the Europeans met in Berlin to carve up Africa among themselves in a mutually agreeable fashion (to each other). With the subsequent "land grab," by 1914 only Liberia and

Ethiopia were able to escape from European control. Land became useful to Europeans not only for the resources found in the land but also for what could be grown on plantations. Products included peanuts, palm oil, cocoa and rubber.

There were various options for Europeans to choose among for governing the constituent lands within their respective empires. Four major forms were available:

- Colonies governed by the respective foreign (i.e. European) power
- Protectorates governed by local bodies under the control of the respective foreign country
- Spheres of Influence were collections of "countries" under a foreign country's power
- Economic Imperialism in which countries were controlled by business units rather than governments

In governing colonies the foreign powers could use indirect or direct methods. With an indirect approach, the foreigners allowed for local control over day-to-day issues. With the direct method, the foreign power ran the government and hence the country. Britain and the US used the indirect method while France and other European countries opted for the direct method.

Africa: The Dark Continent

During the latter part of the 19th century Europeans referred to Africa as the Dark Continent since it was largely unexplored and therefore it was a "mysterious" land. The use of "Dark" referred to the absence of European knowledge about Africa. It is akin to the use of Dark Ages to refer to medieval times (although some scholars object to the use of the term). It is important to understand that the use of the expression was independent of racial attributes of inhabitants, and also had nothing to do with absence of lighting. It is believed that the first written reference was in Henry Stanley's account of his travels in Africa, *Through the Dark Continent.* Many readers may best remember Stanley for his famous question, "Dr. Livingston, I presume?" Another famous work is Joseph Conrad's *Heart of Darkness.*

FIGURE 1: MAP OF AFRICA CIRCA 1914

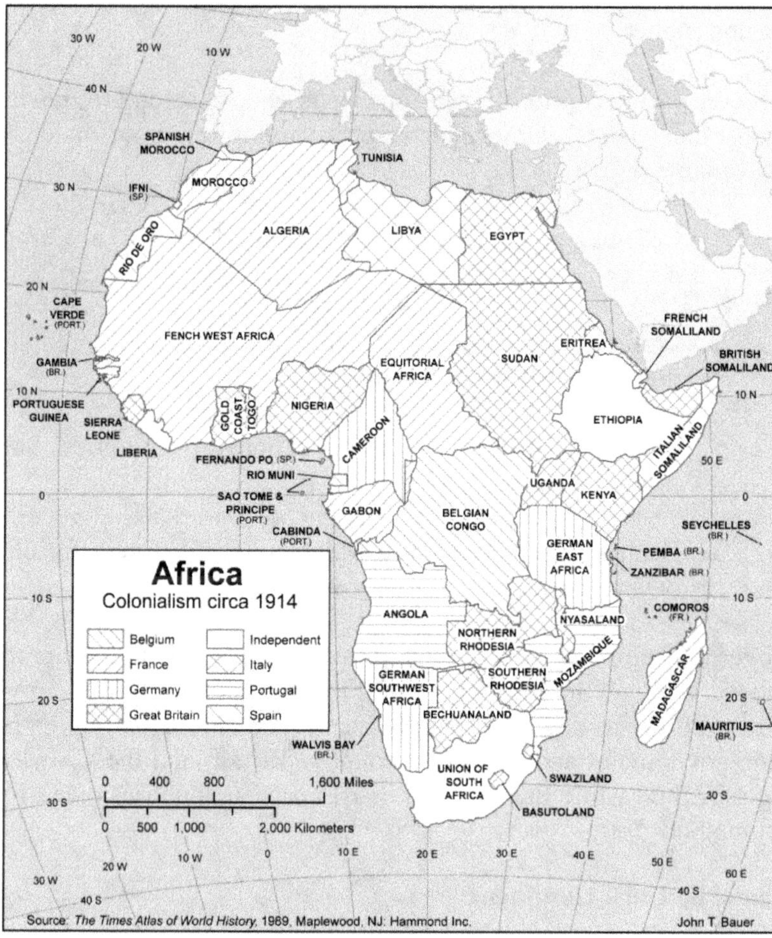

Africa: 1914-1945

...people, especially the youth are no more satisfied with the old order, which admits of little or no progressive adjustments as time goes on.

> --Nnamdi Azikawe, editorial in *The Comet*, December 24, 1936, cited in BBC (Undated II).

Intense political and intellectual change characterized the time between the world wars for the African people. Urban Africans sought more say in affairs. Following WWI, the German colony of Ruanda-Urundi was transferred to Belgium. The Belgians granted favored status to the Tutsis (Draper, 2011). The tensions between the Tutsis and Hutus would fester and eventually flare up in the 1990s (Draper, 2011). With the start of WWII, Africans ceased pushing their grievances and became involved in the war. Having fought for Europe, the Africans felt they had earned the right to self-rule. With India achieving independence in 1947, the push for African independence became relentless. French and British colonial systems collapsed within a 70 year period. Imperialism, while quite brief historically, has had a lasting impact on the African Psyche and economies (BBC, Undated II). Vestiges of this period can be seen in modern times as Africans refer to international policies confronting them, which they dislike, as being evidence of western imperialism.

1960: The Year of Africa

The year 1960 is recognized as "The Year of Africa" since in this year 17 African states received independence from their European rulers. At this time some countries split into two countries, while in other cases new countries were formed through the unification of former colonies. Some were renamed at the time or at subsequent dates.

This new independence was seen as a symbol of coming of age. Free of colonial rule, African states and its peoples looked forward to enhancing the lives of Africans. Mbaku (2003) set out several expectations that Africans had for the post-colonial era. They looked forward to:

a. Democratic (people-driven, participatory and inclusive) constitution-making to provide themselves with dispensations that reflected their customs, realities, beliefs, values, cultures, and aspirations.
b. Public policies focused on the objectives of indigenous peoples.

c. The provision of an enabling institutional environment for the effective management of ethnic diversity.

d. Historical injustices being dealt with.

e. Restructured property rights which would achieve equity in resource allocation and sustainability in resource exploitation.

Unfortunately, these lofty aspirations would not be realized. Mbaku (2003) provides a damning assessment: "During most of the last 50 years in many African countries, regulations such as price controls on agricultural products, interest rate ceilings, foreign exchange controls, and licensing have enriched special interest groups while perpetuating poverty." To these regulatory barriers to economic progress and improvements in human well-being, we can add population pressures, weak governance, corruption, climate threats and civil wars.

2005: (Another?) Year of Africa

The international community declared 2005 as the Year of Africa. The year 2005 saw an "unprecedented global focus on the [African] continent, with significant promises and undertakings made in development and poverty alleviation" (WEF, 2006). Two significant reports emerged in 2005 with special attention on Africa, especially Sub-Saharan Africa (SSA). The Blair Commission Report (2005) was devoted entirely to Africa. The Sachs Report (2005) on the Millennium Development Goals devoted a special section of the Report to issues in SSA. A few years later, the Spence Report (2008) on development also devoted a section of the Report to SSA.

In 2005, the UK assumed the chair position of the G-8 group of industrial countries (the US, the UK, France, Germany, Italy, Canada, Japan, and Russia). The UK Prime Minister made reducing poverty in Africa through development the central pillar of his leadership of the high-level group (WEF, 2006). Consistent with this focus, the aforementioned G8 Summit (Glen Eagles, 2005) concentrated on development issues facing poor countries, and it paid special attention to the difficulties in Africa. The UN's 2005 World Summit, a follow-up to the UN Millennium Summit (UNGA, 2000), reaffirmed the MDGs, and it devoted a section of its report to "Meeting the special needs of Africa" (UNGA, 2005).

The African Peer Review Mechanism started in 2005, and 26 countries signed on for the program. Launched in 2004, the Millennium Challenge Account signed its first agreements in 2005 with Madagascar and Cape Verde, and another country, Benin, in 2006.

Film and Celebrity Attention in the 2000s

A number of films focused on Africa were released during the first decade of the new millennium. We present the following sample:

2001: Black Hawk Down
2003: Tears of the Sun
2004: Hotel Rwanda
2006: Blood Diamond
2006: The Last King of Scotland
2009: Attack on Darfur
2009: Invictus

A number of celebrities have become identified with the African cause especially with the civil war in Darfur in the Sudan. We mention just four individuals, Don Cheadle, George Clooney Mia Farrow, and Angelina Jolie, each of whom has been very visible and an ardent supporter of intervention to stop the strife in Africa.

The theme of this book is that the struggles for development in Sub-Saharan Africa feature good, bad and ugly aspects. Next we highlight some features in each category.

AFRICA: THE GOOD, THE BAD AND THE UGLY

The Good

The SSA region has shown significant improvement in economic growth since 2000. It has tended to be in the middle of the pack of developing regions rather than being the world's economic basket case occupying the bottom position. In 2009, SSA managed to have positive economic growth while most other regions of the world suffered economic contraction. In *The Economist's* 2011 world forecasts, Thaker (2011) predicted that SSA, in 2011, would be one of the fastest growing regions in the world. This prediction is consistent with the IMF's September 2011 projections which lists SSA as the second fastest growing region (behind Developing Asia).

The World Economic Forum on Africa (WEF, 2006) listed the following positive signs for SSA:

- A better governance climate in many SSA countries with a deepening of democracy and successful conclusion of a number of elections
- A new resolve to promote the African business and investment climate
- The tripling of trade with China
- The increase in capital inflows

The Bad

Despite the improved economic growth, poverty and hunger levels in SSA remain considerably higher than desirable. The 2008 *Global Monitoring Report* in its assessment of the progress towards meeting the MDGs observes that "while the MDG1 poverty reduction target will be met at the global level, Sub-Saharan Africa is likely to fall well short. .....At the regional level, Sub-Saharan Africa lags on all MDGs…." (World Bank, 2008). Indeed, only South Asia competes for the lowest ranking for some MDGs; however, even South Asia is expected to meet the poverty reduction goal, MDG1, leaving SSA as the only region of the world to fail to meet the poverty reduction goal.

The improvement in governance holds for some but not all SSA countries. Most countries score poorly on a number of indices related to governance issues. Many elections suffer from various forms of "tampering" which impedes the growth of the desired democracy. This underscores the fact that the existence of electoral processes is not sufficient for a functioning democracy to prevail. Zakaria (2003) discusses democracy versus illiberal democracy in considerable detail.

Civil conflict and civil wars continue to exist, or re-emerge, in many countries. Miguel (2009) comments that: "unless the wars in Congo and Sudan end, they will soon threaten Africa's new democracies and economic success stories."

Infrastructure is lacking or is very poor. China has been assisting various SSA countries in this regard; however, the heavy involvement of China in

SSA may prove to be a very mixed blessing for the countries involved. While China's investments clearly bring benefits in developing Africa's natural resources and infrastructure, some believe it also brings "slave-labor" conditions (Miguel, 2009).

The Ugly

Here we briefly mention two major African "uglies." The first consists of civil war. The civil wars in SSA are particularly gruesome. There have been charges of genocide in Darfur. Rape and other sexual abuse are being used as strategic weapons of war, especially in the Congo. Children are being used as combatants in the hostilities. Millions of people are displaced from their homes each year as a result of war violence impacting them, or from the fear of such violence. These displaced persons, especially women and children, face various severe adverse impacts.

The second concerns the consequences of climate change for Sub-Saharan Africa. Climate change has been identified as the source of drought in the eastern African countries of Djibouti, Ethiopia, Eritrea, Kenya, Somalia and Uganda. The number of people at risk from hunger, according to the UN, was about 12.4 million (Perry, 2011). It became particularly acute in southern Somalia during 2011 which was in famine with 2.8 million people starving or at risk of starving. The situation in Somalia has been made more severe as a result of the Law of Unintended Consequences. The US War on Terror and the campaign against Islamic terrorists worsened the catastrophe as it became increasingly difficult to supply food aid to those most in need (Perry, 2011). The environmental and hunger consequences have resulted in a set of new displaced persons, both as refugees and as internally displaced persons (*TIME*, 2011). These displaced persons are adding to already overcrowded camps, especially in Kenya.

REFERENCES

BBC. Undated I. The Story of Africa: Early History www.bbc.co.uk/worldservice/africa/features/storyofafrica/index_section2.shmtl

BBC. Undated II. The Story of Africa: Between World Wars (1914-1945) www.bbc.co.uk/worldservice/africa/features/storyofafrica/index_section2.shmtl

Commission for Africa (the Blair Commission Report). 2005. *Our Common Interest*, London.

Commission on Growth and Development (the Spence Report). 2008. *The Growth Report: Strategies for Sustained Growth and Inclusive Development.*

Draper, R. 2011. Rift in Paradise. *National Geographic*. November. 83-117.

Feinberg, H.M. and Solodow, J.B. 2002. Out of Africa. *Journal of African History*. 43, 255-261.

Fischman, J. 2011. Part Ape and Part Human. *National Geographic.* August, 120-133.

Henn, B. et al. 2011. Hunter-gatherer genomic diversity suggests a southern Africa origin for modern humans. *Proceedings of the National Academy of Science*. 108(13), 5154-5162.

Loewenberg, S. 2011. Haven and Hell. *TIME.* August 8, 34-42.

Mbaku, J. M. 2003. Entrenching Economic Freedom in Africa. *CATO Journal.* 23(2), 217-225.

Miguel, E. 2009. *Africa's Turn?* MIT Press, Cambridge, MA.

Naik, G. 2011. Clues to Man's First Migration: Genes from Australia Point to Several Waves of African Dispersal, Not Just One. *Wall Street Journal (WSJ)*. 9-23-2011, p. A3.

Perry, A. 2011. A Famine We Made? *TIME*, 9-5-2011, 38-41.

Thaker, P. 2011. South of the Sahara: Boom times, at least in parts. *The World in 2011, The Economist.* 80.

United Nations Development Program (UNDP). 2007. Fighting Climate Change: Human Solidarity in a Divided World. Human Development Report 2007/2008.

United Nations General Assembly (UNGA). 2000. United Nations Millennium Declaration. New York, N.Y.

United Nations General Assembly (UNGA). 2005. 2005 World Summit Outcomes. New York, NY.

United Nations Millennium Project (the Sachs Report). 2005. *Investing in Development: A Practical Plan to Achieve the Millennium Development Goals.*

Willerslev, E. et al. 2011. An Aboriginal Australian Genome Reveals Separate Human Dispersals into Asia. *Science. 9-23-2011, online podcast.*

World Bank. 2008. MGDs and the Environment. Global Monitoring Report 2008. Washington, D.C.

World Economic Forum on Africa. (WEF). 2006. *Going for Growth.* May 31-June 2.

Zakaria, F. 2003. *The Future of Freedom: Illiberal Democracy at Home and Abroad.* Norton. New York, NY.

CHAPTER 3
CLASSIFICATIONS AND FEATURES OF SUB-SAHARAN AFRICAN COUNTRIES

INTRODUCTION

This chapter lists the countries of Sub-Saharan African and their population levels. It also considers selected economic factors, economic/geographic factors, and political factors that impact SSA's ability to enhance human and economic development.

As mentioned above, the framework for promoting human and economic development in the world's poor countries since 2000 is provided by the United Nations Millennium Declaration and the set of Millennium Development Goals (MDGs). It is the consensus of development experts that Sub-Saharan Africa (SSA) is unlikely to meet any of the MDGs by 2015 (the target date for most MDGs). The present chapter does not focus on the MDGs, but rather on selected economic factors, economic/geographic factors, and political factors which may inhibit SSA's ability to achieve the set of Millennium Development Goals by the target date of 2015.

WHAT COUNTRIES FORM SUB-SAHARAN AFRICA?

First, we consider the countries which are included in this region. While defining SSA seems straightforward, the countries which are included under this label depend upon the source to which the reader is referring. PRB (2011) defines SSA as all of Africa except for the countries of North Africa: Algeria, Egypt, Libya, Morocco, Tunisia, and Western Sahara. However, contrary to their own foregoing demarcation, PRB places Sudan in the Northern Africa in the section of its World Population Data Sheets dealing with characteristics of countries in the various regions of the world. The World Bank (2011) excludes Djibouti from SSA and includes it with the Middle East and North African (MENA) group. UNDP (2003) included Djibouti, Somalia, and Sudan with the set of Arab countries rather than SSA. PRB (2011) and the World Bank (2011) include Mayotte in SSA, and PRB includes Reunion in SSA. The *Africa Guide* (Undated) and *countriesandcities.com* (Undated) include Reunion but not Mayotte in their SSA country lists. This book uses the set of SSA countries in Table 1 whenever possible with two exceptions: Reunion will appear in Table 1, and Mayotte will be included in Tables 1 and 2. Neither will appear subsequently since several reports exclude them. In

January 2011 a referendum held in Southern Sudan determined that the country would be divided into two countries in July 2011.These are known as Sudan (in the north) and South Sudan. In the Tables in this book unless otherwise indicated, Sudan refers to the former single country called Sudan.

Table 1: Countries of SSA and North Africa along with their Respective 2011 Population Levels (Arranged by African Geographic Sub-Regions)

		Population (millions)			Population (millions)			Population (millions)
	Western Africa	**313.0**		**Eastern Africa**	**369.0**		**Middle Africa**	**131.0**
1	Benin	9.1	1	Burundi	10.2	1	Angola	19.6
2	Burkina Faso	17.0	2	Comoros	0.8	2	Cameroon	20.1
3	Cape Verde	0.5	3	Djibouti	0.9	3	CAR**	5.0
4	Cote d'Ivoire	22.6	4	Eritrea	5.9	4	Chad	11.5
5	Gambia	1.8	5	Ethiopia	87.1	5	Congo, Rep	4.1
6	Ghana	25.0	6	Kenya	41.6	6	Congo, DR	67.8
7	Guinea	10.2	7	Madagascar	21.3	7	Equatorial Guinea	0.7
8	Guinea-Bissau	1.6	8	Malawi	15.9	8	Gabon	1.5
9	Liberia	4.1	9	Mauritius	1.3	9	Sao Tome and Principe	0.2
10	Mali	15.4	10	Mayotte	0.2			
11	Mauritania	3.3	11	Mozambique	23.1		**Southern Africa**	**58.0**
12	Niger	16.1	12	Reunion	0.9	1	Botswana	2.0
13	Nigeria	162.3	13	Rwanda	10.9	2	Lesotho	2.2
14	Senegal	12.8	14	Seychelles	0.1	3	Namibia	2.3
15	Sierra Leone	5.4	15	Somalia	9.9	4	South Africa	50.5
16	Togo	5.8	16	Sudan*	44.6	5	Swaziland	1.2
			17	Tanzania	46.7			
			18	Uganda	34.5		**North Africa**	168
			19	Zambia	13.5	1	Algeria	36
			20	Zimbabwe	12.1	2	Egypt	82.6
						3	Libya	6.4
						4	Morocco	32.3
						5	Tunisia	10.7
						6	Western Sahara	0.5

Source: PRB (2011). *The author has added Sudan in with SSA. ** CAR is the Central African Republic. CAR will be used throughout the book.

The political geography of modern day Africa is shown on the next page in Figure 2.

Figure 2: Current Map of Africa

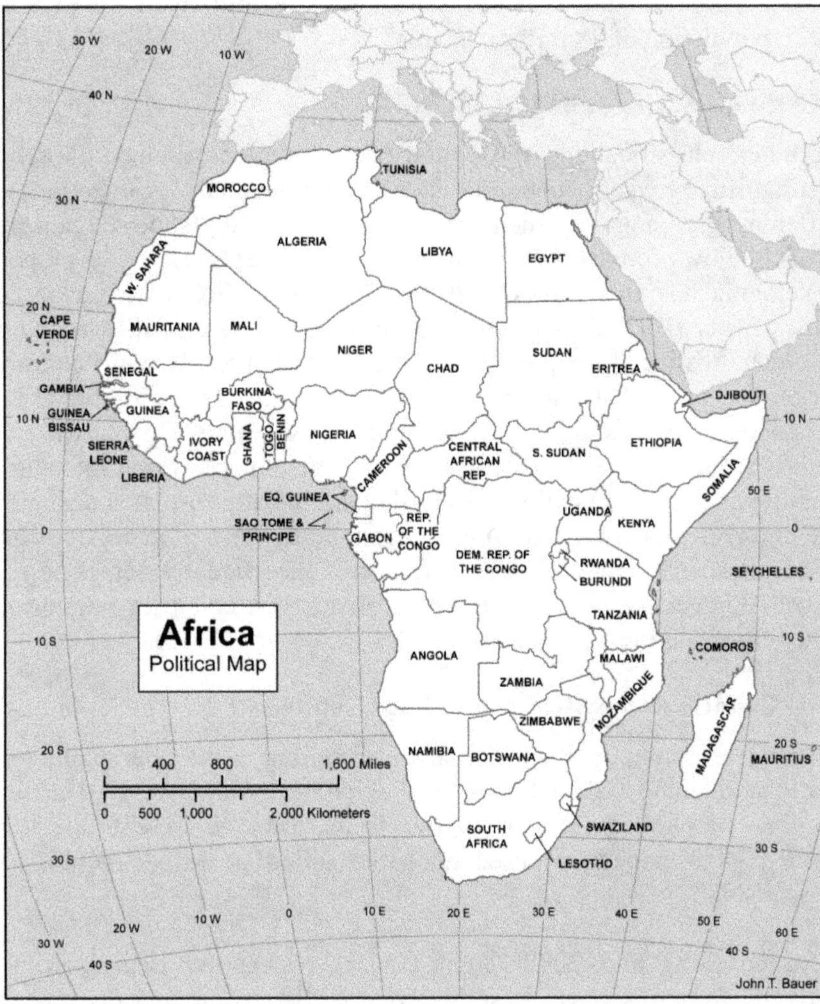

The population size of the SSA countries varies widely from 0.1 million people in the Seychelles to 162.3 million in Nigeria. The median population country (Somalia) has about 9.9 million people (PRB, 2011). The population sizes of the North African countries varies from 0.5 million people in the Western Sahara to 82.6 million in Egypt with a mean population of 28 million people.

ECONOMIC CLASSIFICATIONS

Common classifications for countries and regions include those that distinguish between economic levels. International organizations use different groupings in their reports. The World Trade Organization (WTO) allows countries to self-identify themselves as either developed or developing countries (WTO, 2011a). The International Monetary Fund (IMF) in its *World Economic Outlook* publications classifies economies as either Advanced Economies or Emerging and Developing Economies. According to the IMF, their "classification is not based on strict criteria, economic or otherwise, and it has evolved over time" (IMF, 2010). The "advanced economies" classification has 33 countries which includes the Group of Seven (G7) major advanced countries, the euro area economies, the newly industrialized Asian economies, and "other" advanced economies. All other 150 countries are classified as "emerging and developing economies." All, but one, of the SSA countries falls into the latter classification.

SSA Countries Classified by GNI per Capita

The World Bank classifies economies according to their per capita Gross National Income (GNI) levels. The reference year is revised annually lagging the publication year by two years. Table 2 presents the World Bank (2011) categories based upon the countries' respective 2009 per capita GNI.

Between 2003 and 2008, eight countries (Angola, Cameroon, Cote d'Ivoire, Rep. of Congo, Lesotho, Nigeria, Sao Tome and Principe, and Sudan) moved from Lower Income Country (LIC) status to Lower Middle Income Country (LMC) status. In 2009, SSA had 29 LICs which accounted for about 67% of the 43 LICs globally (World Bank, 2011). Equatorial Guinea moved from LIC status in 2003 to Other High Income status in 2008, and it was the only SSA country with that status in 2011.

Table 2: SSA Countries Classified by GNI per Capita (2009)

LICs (≤ $995)	LICs Cont'd (≤ $995)	LMCs ($996-$3,945)	UMCs ($3,946-$12,195)
1. Benin	16. Madagascar	1. Angola	1. Botswana
2. Burkina Faso	17. Malawi	2. Cameroon	2. Gabon
3. Burundi	18. Mali	3. Cape Verde	3. Mauritius
4. CAR	19. Mauritania	4. Congo, Rep	4. Mayotte
5. Chad	20. Mozambique	5. Cote d'Ivoire	5. Namibia
6. Comoros	21. Niger	6. Djibouti*	6. Seychelles
7. Congo, DR	22. Rwanda	7. Lesotho	7. South Africa
8. Eritrea	23.Sierra Leone	8. Nigeria	
9. Ethiopia	24. Somalia	9. Sao Tome and Principe	**Other High Income (≥ $12,196)**
10. Gambia	25. Tanzania	10. Senegal	1. Equatorial Guinea
11. Ghana	26. Togo	11. Sudan	
12. Guinea	27. Uganda	12. Swaziland	
13. Guinea-Bissau	28. Zambia		
14. Kenya	29. Zimbabwe		
15. Liberia			

Source: World Bank (2011). *Djibouti has been moved from the MENA category to SSA by the authors.

Least Developed Countries (LDCs)

The Least Developed Countries (LDCs) are the sub-set of the Developing Countries group that is comprised of the world's poorest economies. In order to be designated as an LDC, a country must satisfy the following three criteria. Have:

a. A low-income level with a maximum three year average income per capita of $745.
b. weak human resources, and
c. high economic vulnerability

In addition, LDC- candidate countries must have a population level below 75 million people.

Table 3 lists the 33 SSA countries included by the UN in the global set of 49 LDCs. Senegal was added to the LDC group following the 2000 review.

Table 3: Least Developed Countries (LDCs) in SSA, 2010

LDCs	LDCs (cont.)
1. Angola	18. Madagascar
2. Benin	19. Malawi
3. Burkina Faso	20. Mali
4. Burundi	21. Mauritania
5. Central Afr. Rep.	22. Mozambique
6. Chad	23. Niger
7. Comoros	24. Rwanda
8. Congo, DR	25. Sao Tome and Principe
9. Djibouti	26. Senegal
10. Eritrea	27. Sierra Leone
11. Ethiopia	28. Somalia
12. Equatorial Guinea	29. Sudan
13. Gambia	30. Togo
14. Guinea	31. Uganda
15. Guinea-Bissau	32. Tanzania
16. Lesotho	33. Zambia
17. Liberia	

Source: UNOHRLLS (2011)

In order to graduate out of the LDC group, a country must achieve, or exceed, the threshold values of at least two of the membership criteria above, or achieve a per capita GNI level at least twice the threshold. Cape Verde graduated from LDC status in 2007. Equatorial Guinea was approved for graduation in 2009 (UNOHRLLS).

Heavily Indebted Poor Countries (HIPCs)

Heavily Indebted Poor Countries (HIPCs) constitute another special set of poor countries. Of the world's 40 HIPC countries, 33 (82.5%) are in SSA, five (12.5%) are in Latin America or Caribbean, and two (5.0%) in Asia. The SSA countries designated as HIPCs are listed in Table 4.

Table 4: Heavily Indebted Poor Countries in SSA, 2010

Pre-Decision Point	Decision Point	Completion Point	Completion Point (cont.)
Eritrea	Chad	Benin	Malawi
Somalia	Comoros	Burkina Faso	Mali
Sudan	Cote d'Ivoire	Burundi	Mauritania
	Guinea	Cameroon	Mozambique
		CAR	Niger
		Congo, Rep.	Rwanda
		DR Congo	Sao Tome and Principe
		Ethiopia	Senegal
		Gambia	Sierra Leone
		Ghana	Tanzania
		Guinea Bissau	Togo
		Liberia	Uganda
		Madagascar	Zambia

Source: IMF (2010)

The 40 countries in the world identified as HIPCs are eligible for debt relief under the *1996 World Bank – IMF Debt Initiative for Heavily Indebted Poor Countries (HIPC)*. Involvement in the HIPC Initiative involves two steps:

Step One: Decision Point.

To be considered for HIPC status a country must satisfy four conditions:

a. Be eligible to borrow from the World Bank's International Development Agency (IDA) and from the IMF's Extended Credit Facility
b. Face an unsustainable debt burden that cannot be dealt with through traditional debt relief mechanisms
c. Have established a track record of reform and sound policies
d. Have developed a Poverty Reduction Strategy Paper (PRSP).

Three SSA countries have not yet satisfied Step One (column 1) while four SSA countries have satisfied Step One (column 2),

Step Two: Completion Point.

In order to receive the complete package available under the HIPC Initiative, a country must satisfy the following three conditions:

a. Establish a further record of good performance under IMF and World Bank loans
b. Implement key reforms agreed upon at the decision point stage
c. Adopt and implement its PRSP for at least a year. (IMF, 2010)

Twenty-six SSA countries have reached the Completion Point (columns 3 & 4).

CFA franc Countries

The CFA franc zone in Africa was established in 1945 at the time that the Bretton Woods international monetary system came into being. Over time, the membership in the zone has changed. Today there are 14 member-countries, of which 12 are former French-ruled countries. The two non-French members are Guinea - Bissau (Portuguese) and Equatorial Guinea (Spanish). Today CFA stands for *Communaute Financiere Africaine* in French, or *African Financial Community* in English.

While the CFA franc zone is discussed as a single entity, it actually comprises countries in two distinct zones: the West African CFA franc zone and the Central African CFA franc zone.

Table 5 lists the current membership in the two zones and previous members.

Table 5: Current and Former Membership in CFA zones

West African CFA franc	Central African CFA franc	Prior members
Benin	Cameroon	Djibouti
Burkina Faso	Central African Republic	Guinea
Cote d'Ivoire	Chad	Mali (left in 1962 but returned in 1984)
Guinea-Bissau	Republic of the Congo	Reunion
Mali	Equatorial Guinea	Madagascar
Niger	Gabon	Mauritania
Senegal		Saint-Pierre and Miquelon
Togo		

Source: Wikipedia (2011)

Regional Trade Agreements (RTAs)

There are several types of RTAs with each specifying different extents of economic integration. For our purposes we can consider just two types of RTA. One is a Free Trade Agreement (FTA), and the other is a Customs Union (CU). A CU is an FTA with an additional requirement that CU members have a common tariff for non-members. Table 6 lists the RTAs in Africa.

Table 6: Africa's Seven RTAs, Their Types and Membership Sizes

Name	Acronym	Type of RTA	Number of Members
Common Market for Eastern and Southern Africa	COMESA	CU	19
East Africa Community	EAC	CU	5
Economic and Monetary Community of Central Africa	CEMAC	CU	6
Economic Community of West African States	ECOWAS	CU	15
Southern Africa Customs Union	SACU	CU	5
Southern African Development Community	SADC	FTA	16
West African Economic and Monetary Union	WAEMU	CU	8

Source: Table is developed from WTO (2011b)

COMESA has the largest membership. COMESA, ECOWAS, and SADC have considerably larger memberships than the other four RTAs. SACU has only five members, but it is the world's oldest customs union having been founded in 1910 (OUSTR, undated).

ECONOMIC GEOGRAPHY FACTORS

Land-locked Developing Countries (LLDCs) and Coastal Countries

According to UNOHRRLS and the IMF, there are 31 Land-locked Developing Countries (LLDC) world-wide, of which 15 are from SSA, and another 16 SSA countries designated as coastal countries. These two groups of countries are listed in Table 7.

Table 7: Landlocked Developing Countries (LLDCs) and Coastal Countries in SSA

LLDC		Coastal	
1.Botswana	9. Mali	1.Benin	9.Mauritius
2.Burkina Faso	10. Niger	2.Cape Verde	10.Mozambique
3.Burundi	11.Rwanda	3.Comoros	11.Sao Tome and Principe
4.Central Afr. Rep.	12.Swaziland	4.Gambia	12.Senegal
5.Chad	13.Uganda	5.Ghana	13.Seychelles
6.Ethiopia	14. Zambia	6.Guinea Bissau	14.South Africa
7.Lesotho	15. Zimbabwe	7.Kenya	15.Tanzania
8.Malawi		8.Madagascar	16.Togo

Source: UNOHRLLS (2011), IMF (2008)

Land-locked countries face additional hurdles in conducting business globally. Selling goods abroad by sea transport requires the use of port facilities in neighboring countries and possibly other fees associated with moving goods through foreign countries. Similarly, importing goods from abroad creates additional costs.

Defining land-locked countries as those countries which do not have ocean access seems quite intuitive; however, alternatives have been used even for those with coastal access. Sachs (2005) defines as "coastal" those countries for which at least 75% of their population lives within 100 km of the coast. This means that a country with a coastline segment may still be classified with the land-locked countries if less than 75% lives within 100 km of the coast. Sudan and the Democratic Republic of Congo are sometimes treated as non-coastal and placed with LLDCs because a significant number of their respective populations are at long distance from coasts. Notice that these two countries do not appear in Table 5.

However, Eritrea, Djibouti and Somalia do not appear on the list of coastal countries either.

The definition of small varies between research units. The Sachs Report (2005) defines small as countries with less than 40 million people. The Sachs definition includes almost all SSA countries as small. In 2010, only seven countries would not be small according to the Sachs criterion (see Table 1). The Spence Report (2008) considers small countries as those with less than two million people. According to this latter definition, there are 15 small countries in SSA.

Small Island Developing States (SIDS)

Small Island Developing States (SIDS) form a special subset of small countries. Six SSA countries out of 32 world-wide are categorized as SIDS, and are presented in Table 8.

Table 8: Small Island Developing Countries (SIDS) in SSA, 2010

SIDS Countries	SIDS Population (millions)
Cape Verde	0.5
Comoros	0.8
Guinea-Bissau	1.6
Mauritius	1.3
Sao Tome and Principe	0.2
Seychelles	0.1

Source: UNOHRLLS (2011) and Table 1 of this chapter

The six SIDS in Table 8 easily satisfy the Spence condition (and, of course, the Sachs condition). SIDS face special economic difficulties since much of what they need for consumption and production needs to be imported from elsewhere.

The Sahel

The Sahel is a semi-arid tropical savanna eco-region that is the transition between the Sahara Desert in the north and the fertile region to the south. The term Sahel is derived from Arabic and means “cost” or “shore” (SFSA, 2010), or “border” or “margin” (Smith, 2008). Countries in the Sahel cut across Africa from the west coast to the east. The set usually includes (all or parts of) Burkina Faso, Chad, Mali, Mauritania, Niger

(WHO, 2006). Other works use an expanded set which includes eastern countries in the "Horn of Africa": Djibouti, Ethiopia, Eritrea, Kenya, and Somalia (SFSA, 2010; Smith, 2008). The Sahel faces difficult development issues. According to WHO (2006), the Sahel "has been suffering from chronic food shortages caused by economic crisis, poverty, desertification and climate changes" since the early 1970s. In the mid-2000s, the Sahel suffered "unusually poor rainfall," a locust invasion, and avian flu that resulted in a crisis in the poultry industries of Niger and Burkina Faso.

The Rift Valley

Contrast the physical description of the Sahel with that of the Great Rift Valley. "The Rift is rich in rainfall, deep lakes, volcanic soil, and biodiversity" (Draper, 2011). Despite the region's natural beauty and seemingly abundant resources, life is quite brutish. "It [the Rift] is also one of the most densely populated places on Earth. A desperate competition for land and resources-and between people and wildlife-has erupted here with unspeakable violence" (Draper, 2011)

POLITICAL FACTORS

Democratic Rule?

The problem of Africa in general and Uganda in particular is not the people but the leaders who want to overstay in power.

--Yowen Museveni, 1986. (President of Uganda 1986 to present)

SSA countries have increasingly moved to political systems characterized by elections to form governments rather than having dictatorial/military rule. However, the presence of elected governmental bodies may not be the same as democracy. For example, elections may be rigged in a number of ways – a criticism often levied at SSA countries. Those losing an election may well call the election process into question.

There are various examples of flawed election results, but we offer just two examples here. One is the violence that erupted in Kenya following the 2007 election. This violence surprised many people who had considered Kenya to be more politically stable. The second is perhaps the most bizarre example. In the 2010 election in Cote d'Ivoire, the President, Laurent Gbagbo, was defeated by his opponent, Mr. Alassane Ouattara.

Mr. Gbagbo claimed the election results were not valid and refused to step down. He was re-installed as President by his Constitutional Council which declared the election results to be invalid. Thus in late 2010 and 2011 Cote d'Ivoire had two presidents. The international community, including neighboring countries, has supported Mr. Ouattara as the duly elected president and called for Mr. Gbagbo to concede defeat-he refused (Crisis Group, 2011). Cote d'Ivoire then descended into a brutal civil war with people fleeing the area and expanding the number of displaced persons. In the end, Mr. Ouatarra won out with the assistance of UN and French troops. During the violence, about 3000 people were killed and about 500,000 additional persons were displaced from their homes (see Chapter 6 for a discussion of displaced persons).

In what looks like a copy-cat move, Andre Mba Obame declared himself to be the "true" President of Gabon in January 2011 and named a cabinet of 19 ministers. Mr. Obame is the opposition leader, and he and 20 of his supporters requested UN protection.

The African Union issued a statement indicating that it was extremely worried by the multiple African crises which apparently are related to elections and governance issues (BBC 2011).

Table 9: Democracy Ratings for SSA Countries

I. FULL DEMOCRACIES	**IV. AUTHORITARIAN REGIMES**
Botswana	Angola
Cape Verde	Burkina Faso
Ghana	Cameroon
Mauritius	CAR
Namibia	Chad
Sao Tome and Principe	Congo, Rep. of
South Africa	Congo, D.R.
II. FLAWED DEMOCRACIES	Cote d'Ivoire
Benin	Djibouti
Lesotho	Equatorial Guinea
Liberia	Eritrea
Mali	Gabon
Mozambique	Guinea-Bissau
Nigeria	Mauritania
Senegal	Niger
Seychelles	Sudan
Sierra Leone	Swaziland
Somaliland	Togo
Tanzania	Zimbabwe
III. HYBRID REGIMES	**V. FAILED STATE**
Comoros	Somalia
Ethiopia	
Gambia	
Guinea	
Kenya	
Madagascar	
Malawi	
Uganda	
Zambia	

Source: *The Economist* (2010)

Only seven SSA countries receive billing as full democracies, while 19 are classified as authoritarian.

Freedom

Zakaria (2003) points out that democracy itself is not an assurance that people will enjoy freedom. Only nine countries are characterized as Free by Freedom House, while 16 countries are characterized as "Not Free" and these are shown in Table 10.

Table 10: Extent of Freedom of SSA Countries, 2009

Free	Partly Free	Not Free
Benin	Burkina Faso	Angola
Botswana	Burundi	Cameroon
Cape Verde	CAR	Chad
Ghana	Comoros	Congo, DR
Mali	Gambia	Congo, Rep
Mauritius	Guinea- Bissau	Cote d'Ivoire
Namibia	Kenya	Djibouti
Sao Tome and Principe	Lesotho	Equatorial Guinea
South Africa	Liberia	Eritrea
	Madagascar	Ethiopia
	Malawi	Gabon
	Mozambique	Guinea
	Niger	Mauritania
	Nigeria	Rwanda
	Senegal	Somalia
	Seychelles	Sudan
	Sierra Leone	Swaziland
	Tanzania	Zimbabwe
	Togo	
	Uganda	
	Zambia	

Source: Puddington (2011)

Table 11: Regional Patterns of Freedom, 2010

	Free # (%)	Partly Free # (%)	Not Free # (%)
The Americas	24 (69)	10 (29)	1 (3)
Asia-Pacific	16 (41)	15 (38)	8 (21)
Central & Eastern Europe/ Former Soviet Union	13 (45)	9 (31)	7 (24)
MENA	1 (6)	3 (17)	14 (78)
SSA	9 (19)	22 (46)	17 (35)
Western Europe	24 (96)	1(4)	0 (0)

Source: Puddington (2011)

SSA has the largest proportion (46%) of countries listed as Partly Free, and it has the second largest proportion (35%) of countries listed as Not

Free. SSA has the second smallest proportion (9%) of countries listed as Free. The other poor performing region is MENA which includes the Middle East and North Africa.

REFERENCES

The Africa Guide. Undated. African Countries. www.africaguide.com. Retrieved 11-21-2010.

BBC NEWS. 2011. Gabon Opposition Leader Andre Mba Obame Seeks UN Refuge. www.bbc.co.uk/news/world-africa . 1-26-2011. Retrieved 1-26-2011.

Crisis Group. 2011. *Crisis Watch*. January 2011, No.89. www.crisisgroup.org

The Commission on Growth and Development. (Spence Report). 2008. *The Growth Report: Strategies for Sustained Growth and Inclusive Development*.

CountriesAndCities.com. Undated. The Countries of Sub-Sahara Africa. www.countriesandcities.com. Retrieved 11-30-2010.

Draper, R. 2011. Rift in Paradise. *National Geographic*. November. 82-117.

The Economist. 2010. The democracy bug is fitfully catching on. July 24, 47-48

International Monetary Fund (IMF). 2008. Sub-Saharan Africa Typology of Countries. IMF Data Mapper.

International Monetary Fund (IMF). 2010. Debt Relief Under the Heavily Indebted Poor Countries (HIPC) Initiative. www.imf.org.

Office of the United States Trade Representative (OUSTR). Undated. Regional Economic Communities. www.ustr.gov

Population Reference Bureau (PRB). 2011. World Population Data Sheet, 2011.

Puddington, A. 2011. *Freedom in the World 2011: The Authoritarian Challenge to Democracy*. www.freedomhouse.org.

Smith, V. 2008. The Sahel Region. CE397-Transboundary Water Resources.

Syngenta Foundation for Sustainable Agriculture (SFSA). 2010. The Sahel Region. www.syngentafoundation.org . Retrieved 11-12-2010.

United Nations Development Program (UNDP). 2003. Millennium Development Goals: A compact among nations to end poverty. *Human Development Report*. New York, N.Y.

United Nations Millennium Project. (The Sachs Report). 2005. *Investing in Development: A Practical Plan to Achieve the Millennium Development Goals.*

United Nations Office of the High Representative for the Least Developed Countries. 2011. Landlocked Developing Countries and Small Island Developing States (UNOHRLLS).

Wikipedia. 2011. CFA franc. 10-5-2011. http://en.wikipedia.org/wiki/CFA_franc . Retrieved 10-25-2011.

World Bank. 2011. Conflict, Security and Development. *World Development Report 2011.* Washington, D.C.

World Health Organization (WHO). 2006. Sahel Region. Health Action in Crises. October

World Trade Organization (WTO). 2011a. Who are the developing countries in the WTO? www.wto.org

World Trade Organization (WTO). 2011b. Regional Trade Agreements. Updated on October 20, 2011.

Zakaria, F. 2003. *The Future of Freedom: Illiberal Democracy at Home and Abroad.* Norton, New York NY.

CHAPTER 4
POPULATION GROWTH AND ECONOMIC GROWTH PERFORMANCE

POPULATION

Malthus on Population

Thomas Robert Malthus made a significant contribution to the understanding of population growth which still influences thought on the topic although his original predictions did not stand the test of time in the major industrial countries. *An Essay on the Principles of Population*, published in 1798, was his first major contribution on the subject. In simple terms, in Malthus's view it was impossible to affect a permanent increase in a society's material well-being beyond the subsistence level. Malthus reasoned that any increase in the standard of living would result in an increase in population that would set in motion forces which cause the society to be pushed back to the subsistence level.

Malthus set forth two postulates to anchor his "theory":

1. Food is necessary to the existence (subsistence) of man, and
2. The passion between the sexes is necessary and will remain nearly in its present state.

Also he had two hypotheses:

i. "population, when unchecked, increases at a geometric rate," and
ii. "subsistence (food production) increases only in an arithmetical ratio."

A couple of simple equations may help in understanding the difference between i and ii. Let P_t denote the size of the population at time t. Population growing at a geometric rate may be represented by an equation like

i(a). $P_{t+1} = a(P_t)^2$.

In i(a) P_{t+1} increases at an increasing, or nonlinear, rate. An arithmetic example provides further insight. For convenience, set a=1, and at t=0, let $P_0 = 2$. Then $P_1 = 4$, $P_2 = 16$, and $P_3 = 256$, and so on.

Letting subsistence at time be S_t, then subsistence growing at an arithmetic rate may be represented by be an equation like

ii(a). $S_{t+1} = b(S_t)$.

In ii(a), S_{t+1} increases at a constant, or linear, rate. For convenience, set b=2, and at t=0, let $S_0 = 1$. Then, $S_1 = 2$, $S_2 = 4$, $S_3 = 8$, and so on.

Malthus postulated that population growth was subject to several checks which constrain the growth. These he grouped into "preventative" and "positive" checks.

Preventative checks consist of factors which result in reductions in fertility. Malthus believed that such checks were vice except for "moral restraint" which is introduced in a later work. Most of the preventative checks involve sexual-related issues that constrain conception.

Positive checks consist of factors which shorten the duration of life. Malthus believed that positive checks are brought about by vice and result in misery. These include extreme poverty, unwholesome occupations, diseases and epidemics, wars, plague and famine.

Agrarian societies were characterized by high birth rates (35 to 55 per 1000) and high mortality rates (30 to 40 per 1000) with recurrent spikes in the mortality rates. With industrialization, the recurrent mortality spikes almost disappear.

Malthus was unable to foresee the changes that would take place over the next two centuries due to the Industrial Revolution which was just in its nascent stages. His views were more suited to an agrarian-based economy which was giving way to industrialization. As a result Malthus's theory today seems more appropriate to SSA than to developed countries.

A Brief Look at World Population Growth "Since the Beginning of Time"

The world has experienced phenomenal changes in population size and composition, especially since the mid-twentieth century. These demographic shifts will significantly affect global economic activity. At the time Malthus was writing his Essay, the world population is estimated to have reached about one billion people. By 1930 the world's population had doubled to two billion. In another 30 years the population had expanded to three billion. Astoundingly, the time for the population to grow from three billion to four billion was only half the time to grow from two to three billion (i.e. 15 years)! Going from four billion to seven billion occurred in three 12 year intervals. In mid-2011, the world's population was 6.99 billion people, and reached seven billion in late 2011 (PRB, 2011). It is the speed-up in population growth observed during the 1960s that resulted in the concern for overpopulation.

Table 1: World Population Growth

World Population Size (billions)	Year Achieved (by year's end)	Years Between Billions
1	1800	All of human history
2	1930	130
3	1960	30
4	1975	15
5	1987	12
6	1999	12
7	2011	12

Sources: McFalls (2007), PRB (2011)

Global Population Trends 1900-2011

Table 2 gives a time profile of population growth by world regions. In the first half of the 20th century, the world's population expanded by 870 million from 1.65 billion to 2.52 billion. In the second half of the century the growth was four times as large, adding about 3.6 billion people. The bulk of this population growth between 1950 and 2000 took place in the less developed countries with these countries almost tripling in size from 1.7 billion to 4.9 billion people.

The Developing Country share of world population in 1950, about 68%, was pretty much the same as it was in 1900 (67%). In 2011 however, the developing countries share was 82% of the global population. Africa's population more than tripled in the last half of the 20th century from 221 million to 1,051 million people, leading the African share of world population to increase from 8/9% in 1900/1950 to 15% in 2011.

Ninety-seven percent of current world population growth is occurring in developing countries. In mid-2011, the world population was roughly

6.99 billion with 5.4 billion living in developing countries. The African population was 1,051 million people with 933 million people living in SSA (defined broadly).

Table 2: Population Profiles in Major World Regions 1900, 1950, 2000 and 2011

Region	1900		1950		2000		2011	
	Million	%	Million	%	Million	%	Million	%
World	1,650	100	2,519	100	6,071	100	6,987	100
Developed Countries	539	33	813	32	1,194	20	1,242	18
Developing Countries	1,111	67	1,706	68	4,877	80	5,745	82
Africa	113	8	221	9	796	13	1,051	15

Source: PRB (2004), PRB (2011)

Table 3 provides information dealing with regional demographic characteristics.

Table 3: Demographic Data for the World, Developed and Developing Countries, and SSA

	Population mid-2011 Millions	Births per 1,000	Deaths per 1,000	Natural Increase %	Total Fertility Rate (TFR) # per woman	Percent of Population < 15 years of age	Percent of Population > 65 years of age
World	6,987	20	8	1.2	2.5	27	8
Developed countries.	1,242	11	10	0.2	1.7	16	16
Developing countries	5,745	22	8	1.4	2.6	29	6
SSA	**928**	**38**	**13**	**2.6**	**5.2**	**43**	**3**

Source: PRB (2011)

As revealed in Table 3, in 2011, SSA is poised for more growth as a result of its higher total fertility rate (TFR, roughly the number of children women have during their lifetime), a greater excess of births over deaths, and a larger natural rate of increase than the group of developing countries. Eberstadt (2010) suggested that SSA would be the man-power growth center in the future replacing China and India in this role. The SSA population is projected to increase to more than 1.2 billion people by 2025 and to over 2 billion by 2050. It has been suggested that "about half of the 2.3 billion increase in the world's population over the next 40 years will be in Africa" (*The Economist,* 2011).

Total Fertility Rates

The TFR that will hold a population stationary (the replacement rate) is generally taken to be 2.1 for developed countries and about 2.3 for developing countries. Intuitively, one would think that replacement would require a TFR of two since this allows a couple to replace themselves with two children. However, despite the intuition, a higher TFR is needed for replacement. Two issues: first, more boys are born than girls (about 105 boys for each 100 girls), and second, not all newborns will survive through the reproductive ages. Countries with TFRs above 2.1(or 2.3) will grow, while those with TFRs below 2.1 (or 2.3) will ultimately decline unless the TFR increases.

Table 3 also shows the stark contrast between the age distributions of the populations in developed countries and those in developing counties. Developed countries are aging more. The developing countries have a much larger proportion of young people. The situation for SSA is particularly striking, with over 40% of the population being under age 15, and only 3% over age 65.

Table 4 contains further information on country specific TFRs for those countries with the highest TFRs.

Table 4: Countries with TFRs of 6.0 or Above, and TFRs of SSA and of the Sets of Least Developed and Developed Countries

	Total Fertility Rate (TFR)
Niger	7.0
Mali	6.4
Somalia	6.4
Uganda	6.4
Burundi	6.4
Zambia	6.3
Congo, D.R.	6.1
Chad	6.0
Sub-Saharan Africa	5.2
Afghanistan	6.3
Least Developed Countries	4.5
Developed Countries	1.7

Sources: PRB (2011)

Other than the eight SSA countries, only Afghanistan has a TFR in excess of 6.0.

ECONOMIC GROWTH PERFORMANCE

SSA has shown marked improvement in its economic growth performance over the last 30 years or so. In the 1986 – 1995 time period, the SSA annual real GDP growth rate of 1.9% exceeded only that of Central and Eastern Europe, and the SSA rate was only about one-quarter of that in Developing Asia. For the 1996 – 2005 period, the SSA annual growth rate is projected to exceed those of Central and Eastern Europe, CIS, and Western Hemisphere regions.

Table 5: Annual Percentage Growth in Real GDP

Region	1986 - 1995	1996 - 2005
Africa	**1.9**	**3.9**
Central & Eastern Europe	0.8	3.5
CIS	- -	3.7
Developing Asia	7.7	6.6
Middle East	2.8	4.5
Western Hemisphere	2.8	2.5

Source: IMF (2004)

Table 6: Annual Percentage Growth in Real GDP per Capita

Region	1975 - 2005	1990-2005
SSA	**- 0.5**	**0.5**
Arab States	0.7	2.3
East Asia & Pacific	6.1	5.8
Latin American & Caribbean	0.7	1.2
South Asia	2.6	3.4
Central & Eastern Europe & CIS	1.4	1.4

Source*:* UNDP (2007)

Table 6 shows the dramatic shift in per capita GDP growth between the time period 1975-2005 and the inter-period, 1990-2005. All regions, except East Asia &Pacific, improved during the latter time period, or remained constant (Central & Eastern Europe and CIS).

The Sachs Report (2005) observed that small remote inland economies performed less well over the 1980-98 time period than large or coastal countries. Most SSA countries fall into the former category.

Output Volatility

The April 2005 *World Economic Outlook* (IMF, 2005) in the discussing output volatility in developing regions, determined that the countries of SSA had the highest volatility of all the regions over the 1970-2003 time-period. Within SSA, the CFA countries had the highest volatility from 1979 – 1990 but have shown a sustained decline in volatility since the mid-1980s. Volatility in non-CFA countries in SSA has reduced somewhat since the 1990s but is still the highest in the regions.

The IMF's (2005) dynamic factor analysis separates contributions to output volatility into global, regional and country-specific factors. For SSA, country- specific factors accounted for over three-quarters of the volatility (76.1% for CFA countries and 82.1% for non-CFA ones). Regional factors are the second major set of factors accounting for 18.2% of CFA volatility which is noticeably higher than the 10.2% non-CFA country volatility. Global factors contribute 5.7% in CFA countries and 6.8% in non-CFA ones. For comparison, the averages for all developing countries are: global, 9.3%; regional, 16.9%; country-specific, 73.8%.
The IMF (2005) notes that research suggests that output volatility may reduce long-term growth and that "investment plays a critical role in

transmitting the negative impact of volatility to growth in Africa." IMF (2011) observed that "almost three years after the [2008/09] crisis, the global economy continues to be challenged with intermittent volatility."

Relative Economic Performance, 1993-2011

Table 7 shows the relative performance of various regions during the 2000s compared to their average performance 1993-2002.

Table 7: Real GDP Growth in Emerging and Developing Economies and Advanced Economies

REGION	AVG 1993-2002	2003	2004	2005	2006	2007	2008	2009	2010	2011*Est.
CEE	3.2	4.8	7.3	5.8	6.4	5.5	3.1	- 3.6	4.5	4.3
CIS	-1.2	7.7	8.1	6.7	8.9	8.9	5.3	- 6.4	4.6	4.6
DA	7.1	8.1	8.5	9.5	10.3	11.5	7.7	7.2	9.5	8.2
MENA	3.3	7.3	5.9	5.4	6.0	6.7	4.6	2.6	4.4	4.0
SSA	3.7	4.9	7.1	6.2	6.4	7.1	5.6	2.8	5.4	5.2
LAC	2.7	2.1	6.0	4.6	5.6	5.8	4.3	- 1.7	6.1	4.5
AE	2.8	1.9	3.1	2.7	3.1	2.8	0.1	- 3.7	3.1	1.6
World	3.3	3.6	4.9	4.6	5.3	5.4	2.8	-0.7	5.1	4.0

Source: IMF (2011)

a) CEE: Central and Eastern Europe, b) CIS: Commonwealth of Independent States, DA: Developing Asia, d) MENA: Middle East and North Africa, e) SSA: Sub-Saharan Africa

Table 8: Real GDP Growth Rates for Selected Groups of SSA Countries

	2007	2008	2009	2010	2011*
SSA (overall)	**7.1**	**5.6**	**2.8**	**5.4**	**5.2**
Oil Exporters	---	---	---	**7.3**	**6.0**
Nigeria	7.0	6.0	7.0	8.7	6.9
Angola	22.6	13.8	2.4	3.4	3.7
Equatorial Guinea	21.4	10.7	5.7	-0.8	7.1
Gabon	5.6	2.3	-1.4	5.7	5.6
Republic of Congo	- 1.6	5.6	7.5	8.8	5.0
Chad	0.2	1.7	-1.2	13.0	2.5
Middle-Income	---	---	---	**3.1**	**3.5**
South Africa	5.6	3.6	-1.7	2.8	3.4
Botswana	4.8	3.0	-4.9	7.2	6.2
Mauritius	5.8	5.5	3.0	4.2	4.2
Namibia	5.4	4.3	-0.7	4.8	3.6
Swaziland	2.0	3.1	1.2	2.0	-2.1
Cape Verde	8.6	6.2	3.7	5.4	5.6
Low-Income	---	---	---	**5.8**	**5.9**
Ethiopia	11.8	11.2	10.0	8.0	7.5
Kenya	7.0	1.5	2.6	5.6	5.3
Ghana	6.5	8.4	4.0	7.7	13.5
Tanzania	6.9	7.3	6.7	6.4	6.1
Cameroon	3.4	2.6	2.0	3.2	3.8
Uganda	8.4	8.7	7.2	5.2	6.4
Cote d'Ivoire	1.6	2.3	3.8	2.4	-5.8

Source: IMF (2011) *Estimated

Oil Exporters as a group outperformed the SSA overall and the Middle and Low Income groups The SSA overall and the Low Income countries outperformed the Middle Income group. The Low Income group does better than the Middle Income group because the Low Income group starts from such a low GDP level. The Oil Exporters do especially well due to favorable market conditions.

REFERENCES

Eberstadt, N. 2010. The Demographic Future: What Population Growth – and Decline Means for the Global Economy. *Foreign Affairs*. 89(6), 54-64.

The Economist. 2011. A tale of three islands. October 22, 2011. 28-30.

International Monetary Fund (IMF). 2004. Advancing Structural Reforms. *World Economic Outlook*, April.

International Monetary Fund (IMF). 2005. Globalization and Economic Balances. *World Economic Outlook*, April.

International Monetary Fund (IMF). 2011. Slowing Growth, Rising Risks. *World Economic Outlook*, September.

Malthus, T.R. 1798. *An Essay on the Principle of Population*. J. Johnson, in St. Paul's Churchyard, London.

McFalls, J.A. 2007. Population: A Lively Introduction. *Population Bulletin*, 62(1). Population Reference Bureau. Washington D.C.

Population Reference Bureau (PRB). 2004. Transitions in World Population. *Population Bulletin*. 59(1).Washington D.C.

Population Reference Bureau (PRB). 2011. World Population Data Sheet, 2011. Washington D.C.

United Nations Development Program (UNDP). 2007. Fighting Climate Change: Human Solidarity in a Divided World. *Human Development Report 2007/2008.*

United Nations General Assembly (UNGA), 2000. United Nations Millennium Declaration.

United Nations Millennium Project (the Sachs Report). 2005. *Investing in Development: A Practical Plan to Achieve the Millennium Development Goals*.

CHAPTER 5
GOVERNANCE, FAILING STATES, AND CIVIL CONFLICT

GOOD GOVERNANCE

Governance is fundamental to development and economic growth.

--*Atlas of Global Development*, (World Bank, 2009)

Governments may fail either because they do too little, or because they do too much.

--Sir Arthur Lewis, *The Theory of Economic Growth*, 1955, (cited in the Spence Report, 2008)

The general consensus of researchers and international organizations is that the major reason for poor economic and human development performance in developing countries is poor governance within those poor performing countries. The *Atlas of Global Development* (World Bank, 2009) provides the following succinct definition of governance:

> **Governance** describes the way public officials and institutions acquire and exercise authority to provide public goods and services, including education, health care, infrastructure, and a sound investment climate.

It adds that "good governance is associated with increased citizen participation and improved accountability of public officials."

It is probably obvious that the distinction between good governance and bad governance is not a simple binary one. Instead, like the notions of fuzzy mathematics, it is one of varying degrees. Consequently, in order to discuss governance, a quantitative measure is desirable. Absent quantitative indicators, the discussions of governance are rather like discussions of beauty—very subjective and frequently relying upon unstated preferences of the discussants.

Indices of Governance

One governance indicator, the ***Country Policy and Institutional Assessment (CPIA)*** index, was developed in the 1970s by the World Bank to assist decision making in the allocation of funding from the International Development Association (IDA). The CPIA is comprised of 16 criteria grouped into the following 4 categories, or clusters:

A. Economic Management
B. Structural Policies
C. Policies for Social Inclusion/Exclusion
D. Public Sector Management and Institutions

Another index, the **Ibrahim Index of African Governance** deals only with African countries (actually just those in Sub-Saharan Africa). The Ibrahim Index, developed in the early to mid-2000s, uses 57 criteria grouped into the following 5 categories:

A. Safety and Security
B. Rule of Law, Transparency and Corruption
C. Participation and Human Rights
D. Sustainable Economic Opportunity
E. Human Development

FAILING OR WEAK STATES

Definitions of State Weakness and State Failure

Deviations from what is viewed as good versus poor governance in countries leads to discussions of "**weak,**" **"fragile" or "failing"** states. Some researchers use these labels as interchangeable (OECD, 2008) while others use one or the other often without specifying the rules for inclusion/exclusion.

The World Bank (2007) offers the following definition of fragile states. ***Fragile States*** are

> countries that are facing particularly severe development challenges such as weak governance, limited administrative capacity, violence, or the legacy of conflict.

This definition is qualitative but does not provide sufficient direction as to which countries are to be included and which are to be excluded by the analyst. For example, how weak does a country's governance have to be for inclusion as a weak or fragile state? The World Bank operationalizes the concept of fragile states by using its country CPIA scores. The categorization is determined by the selection of an appropriate cutoff value for the CPIA below which countries are deemed to be fragile states. For the cutoff points, the World Bank adopted its criteria for classifying countries as **Low Income Countries under Stress** (LICUS) for the allocation of funding. **Fragile states** are defined as those countries with CPIA scores below 3.0, and those with CPIA scores between 3.0 and 3.2 are deemed to be **marginally fragile**. Using these values, in 2005, there were 30 fragile states of which 16 are in SSA, and nine marginally fragile states of which seven are in SSA. Since the states are reported alphabetically rather than in CPIA rank order, it is not possible to ascertain which countries are in more dire situations.

Foreign Policy and the Fund for Peace (FP/FfP) use 12 criteria to produce their ***Failed States Index 2010*** (using 2009 data) which ranks 177 countries relative to weakness or vulnerability. The bottom 30 states include 16 SSA countries.

Rice and Patrick (2008) introduce another definition of weak states and a new index for assessment. They define ***Weak States*** as:

> countries that lack the essential capacity and/or will to fulfill four sets of critical government responsibilities: fostering an environment conducive to sustainable and equitable economic growth; establishing and maintaining legitimate, transparent, and accountable political institutions; securing their populations from violent conflict and controlling their territory; and meeting the basic human needs of their population.

The Rice and Patrick ***Index of State Weakness in the Developing World*** ranks 141 developing countries relative to their performance in the four critical areas in the above definition.

Statistical Summaries of State Governance, or State Weakness/Failure

Results for the four indices discussed in this section are summarized in Table 1, along with an early subjective assessment by Rotberg (2002). In these rankings, a 1 denotes the poorest governance or the most fragile or failing country.

Table 1: Recent Indices of SSA Governance, Fragile/Weak States and Rotberg's 2002 Qualitative Assessment (ascending order)

Rank	FP/FfP Failed States Index 2008 (bottom 16)	Rice's and Patrick's Index of State Weakness 2008 (bottom 16)	World Bank's CPIA 3.0 and Below 2007 (bottom 16 in alphabetical order)	Ibrahim Index African Governance 2009 (Bottom 10)	Rotberg's 2002 Subjective Assessment of State Failure
1	Somalia	Somalia	Angola	Somalia	Somalia
2	Sudan	Congo, DR	Burundi	D.R. Congo	Angola
3	Zimbabwe	Burundi	CAR	Chad	Burundi
4	Chad	Sudan	Chad	Sudan	Congo, DR
5	Congo, DR	CAR	Comoros	Angola	Liberia
6	Cote d'Ivoire	Zimbabwe	D.R. Congo	CAR	Sierra Leone
7	CAR	Liberia	Rep. of Congo	Cote d'Ivoire	Sudan
8	Guinea	Cote d'Ivoire	Cote d'Ivoire	Eritrea	
9	Ethiopia	Angola	Eritrea	Guinea	
10	Uganda	Sierra Leone	Guinea	Nigeria	
11	Nigeria	Eritrea	Guinea- Bissau		
12	Niger	Chad	Liberia		
13	Burundi	Guinea-Bissau	Somalia		
14	Rep. of Congo	Ethiopia	Sudan		
15	Kenya	Rep. of Congo	Togo		
16	Malawi	Niger	Zimbabwe		

Consider first the rankings of the results of the Indices. Recall that the World Bank's CPIA-rank order is alphabetical rather than according to individual country scores. This means that the CPIA ordering is not comparable to the other indices. For the three other indices there is considerable agreement. Consider the bottom 10 for the FP/FfP. Six of the Rice and Patrick bottom 10 are also in FP/FfP, and seven of the Ibrahim bottom 10 appear in the FP/FfP bottom 10. Somalia has the worst performance in each of the lists. FP/FfP and Rice and Patrick refer to Somalia as a failed state. Rotberg's seven countries are all in the Rice and Stewart bottom 10 despite being based upon an earlier time reference. Rotberg went further and termed Somalia "the model of a **collapsed state**."

Table 1 lists country performance across different indices, and Tables 2 and 3 list country performances in different years for given indices.

Table 2: Country "Failure" Rankings for 2008, 2010 and 2011: FP/FfP Index

Rank 2008	FP/FfP Failed States Index 2008	Rank 2010	FP/FfP Failed States Index 2010	Rank 2011	FP/FfP Failed States Index 2011
1	Somalia	1	Somalia	1	Somalia
2	Sudan	2	Chad	2	Chad
3	Zimbabwe	3	Sudan	3	Sudan
4	Chad	4	Zimbabwe	4	Congo, DR
5	Congo, DR	5	Congo, DR	5	Zimbabwe
6	Cote d'Ivoire	6	CAR	6	CAR
7	CAR	7	Guinea	7	Guinea
8	Guinea	8	Cote d'Ivoire	8	Cote d'Ivoire
9	Ethiopia	9	Kenya	9	Nigeria
10	Uganda	10	Nigeria	10	Niger

Source: *Foreign Policy* (2008, 2010, 2011)

Eight of 10 countries appear in each year's index albeit with changes in order. Ethiopia and Uganda drop off in the second year and were replaced by Kenya and Nigeria. In the third year Kenya is replaced by Niger. The worst five countries in each year are the same. Of course, Somalia anchors each year in the most failed spot.

In Table 3, eight show up in each year. In year 2, Angola and Nigeria drop out and are replaced by Equatorial Guinea and Zimbabwe. In the third year, Guinea is replaced by Guinea-Bissau. Again the most- failed country position is occupied by Somalia.

In a listing of the 23 worst dictators, 11 were from SSA countries (Ayittey, 2010) and Nigeria was listed as one of four countries in "big trouble," hence it appears on the Watch List (Dickenson, 2010). In the *Foreign Policy* list of the top 10 failed states, SSA accounted for seven of the 10.

Table 3: Country "Failure" Rankings for 2008, 2010 and 2011: Ibrahim Index

Rank in the 2009 Index	Ibrahim Index African Governance 2009	Rank in the 2010 Index	Ibrahim Index African Governance 2010	Rank in the 2011 Index	Ibrahim Index African Governance 2011
1	Somalia	1	Somalia	1	Somalia
2	D.R. Congo	2	Chad	2	Chad
3	Chad	3	DR Congo	3	Zimbabwe
4	Sudan	4	Eritrea	4	Congo, DR
5	Angola	5	Zimbabwe	5	CAR
6	CAR	6	CAR	6	Sudan
7	Cote d'Ivoire	7	Sudan	7	Eritrea
8	Eritrea	8	Equatorial Guinea	8	Cote d'Ivoire
9	Guinea	9	Guinea	9	Equatorial Guinea
10	Nigeria	10	Cote d'Ivoire	10	Guinea-Bissau

Source: Ibrahim Index (2009, 2010, 2011)

Corruption

Poor governance and corruption are likely to lead to state failure whereby countries lose the capacity to deliver on appropriate services. A measure of a well-functioning democracy with good governance is the level of corruption indicated by the Corruption Perceptions Index (CPI).

The Corruption Perceptions Index (CPI)

The CPI ranges from 0.0 (highly corrupt) to 10.0 (very clean). Of 178 countries covered in the 2009 CPI global study, almost 75% had a CPI below 5. According to Transparency International (2009), "these results indicate a serious corruption problem." In 2011, 72% of countries globally had CPIs less than 5.0.

Table 4 lists measures of countries rated as the most corrupt for 2009, 2010 and 2011 defined as those with CPIs less than or equal to 2.5, a cutoff that is somewhat arbitrary.

Table 4: SSA Countries with CPIs Less Than or Equal to 2.5

2009		2010		2011	
Country	**CPI**	**Country**	**CPI**	**Country**	**CPI**
Somalia	1.1	Somalia	1.1	Somalia	1.0
Sudan	1.5	Sudan	1.6	Sudan	1.6
Chad	1.6	Chad	1.7	Equatorial Guinea	1.9
Burundi	1.8	Burundi	1.8	Burundi	1.9
Equatorial Guinea	1.8	Equatorial Guinea	1.9	DR Congo	2.0
Guinea	1.8	Angola	1.9	Chad	2.0
Angola	1.9	Guinea	2.0	Angola	2.0
DR Congo	1.9	DR Congo	2.0	Guinea	2.1
Guinea-Bissau	1.9	Kenya	2.1	Zimbabwe	2.1
Rep. Congo	1.9	Guinea-Bissau	2.1	Kenya	2.2
CAR	2.0	Rep. Congo	2.1	Guinea-Bissau	2.2
Cote d'Ivoire	2.1	Cote d'Ivoire	2.2	Cote d'Ivoire	2.2
Cameroon	2.2	Cameroon	2.2	Rep Congo	2.2
Sierra Leone	2.2	Mauritania	2.3	CAR	2.2
Zimbabwe	2.2	Zimbabwe	2.4	Uganda	2.4
Comoros	2.3	Togo	2.4	Togo	2.4
Mauritania	2.5	Sierra Leone	2.4	Nigeria	2.4
Nigeria	2.5	Nigeria	2.4	Mauritania	2.4
Mozambique	2.5	Uganda	2.5	Comoros	2.4
Uganda	2.5			Sierra Leone	2.5
				Niger	2.5
				Eritrea	2.5
				Cameroon	2.5

Source: Transparency International (2009, 2010 and 2011)

The two most corrupt SSA countries for 2009-2011 were Somalia and Sudan. The third worst was Chad in 2009 and 2010, but this rank was taken by Equatorial Guinea in 2011. In each year, Burundi ranks as fourth worst. Position five is held by Equatorial Guinea in 2009 and 2010, but in 2011 it is held by DR Congo. While there are some rank changes the five most corrupt SSA countries in the three years, there is only one new country in the worst five in 2011, DR Congo.

Only three SSA countries have a CPI greater than five in either year. For SSA, 93% had a CPI below 5.0—an even more serious problem than exists globally! Only five have a score between 4.0 and 5.0 in 2010, and only three in 2009 and in 2011. In 2011, three had CPIs of 5.0 or higher.

Kenya had an index of 2.1 in 2010 and 2.2 in 2009. The Kenyan government has suggested that corruption could be costing it almost one third of its national budget (Mwachiro, 2010).

Most attention on corruption is on what might be called "big-time corruption" in which, for example, kick-backs may be demanded by senior government officials to assist some individual, enterprise or other group in achieving some desired end. The World Bank (2011) introduces the term "quiet corruption" to capture the more subtle losses due to inaction on the part of service providers.

Poverty Gap

Not all researchers believe that weak governance is the major factor in producing poor performance. In its assessment of progress towards meeting the MDGs, the Sachs Report (2005) devotes a separate chapter to "Africa's special needs." While stating that "The standard diagnosis of Africa is that the continent is suffering from a governance crisis," the Sachs Report is adamant that the problem is deeper— "Governance is an issue, but Africa's development challenges are much deeper." The Sachs Report (2005) argued that "there is no evidence that Africa's governance, on average is worse than elsewhere once we control for Africa's low income." The root problem according to the Sachs Report is the African **poverty trap**.

The following structural reasons for vulnerability to the poverty trap are offered by the Report:

- Very high transport costs and small markets
- Low- productivity agriculture
- Very high disease burden
- A history of adverse geopolitics
- Very slow diffusion of technology from abroad.

The World Bank (2005) directly challenged the Sachs conclusion that the cause of the Sub-Saharan Africa situation is a poverty trap, asserting instead that there is "no systematic evidence supporting the empirical relevance of poverty traps." The World Bank (2005) supports the view that "improving governance is the biggest challenge facing developing countries," and furthermore, that "the perception that economic governance is weaker in Sub-Saharan Africa than in other regions is broadly supported by available indicators." Counter to the Sachs Report conclusion, The World Bank (2005) states that "empirical evidence suggests that the stronger causality effect is from governance to income and, once that is accounted for, most African countries have governance scores lower than would be expected on the basis of their income levels."

The Blair Commission Report (2005) views improvement in governance in Africa to be the main need—"Without progress in governance, all other reforms will have limited impact." This view is shared by other assessments such as the Monterrey Consensus, "good governance is essential for sustainable development." UNDP (2003) states that "Governance, the policies and institutions that regulate interactions among individuals and groups in society, is seen as part of the foundation for sustained growth and human development."

In Tables 1, 2 and 3 above, the focus was on the poorest performers. In Table 5, the focus is on the top 10 performers on the FP/FfP and Ibrahim indices.

Table 5: Best Governance Performers in SSA, 2011 Indices

Rank	FP/FfP Index	Ibrahim Index
1	Djibouti	Mauritius
2	Madagascar	Cape Verde
3	Mozambique	Botswana
4	Comoros	Seychelles
5	Zambia	South Africa
6	Angola	Namibia
7	Mauritania	Ghana
8	Equatorial Guinea	Lesotho
9	Burkina Faso	Benin
10	Togo	Sao Tome and Principe

Sources: *Foreign Policy* (2011), Ibrahim Foundation (2011)

When good governance performance is assessed there is no country which appears on both lists!

CIVIL CONFLICT

The most extreme breakdown of governance is war.

--The Blair Commission (2005)

Between 1945 and 1977, about 80% of the victims of armed conflicts were a result of non-international conflicts (ICRC, 2006). Collier (2000) noted that 25 of 27 major armed conflicts in 1999 were civil conflicts.

Researchers note that conflict is both a cause of countries becoming fragile, and an outcome of the low economic performance in fragile states (UNDP, 2007). Nafziger and Auvinen (2002) found "that the incidence of conflict in Africa exceeded the incidence in other developing regions of the world in the 1990s," and the number of deaths in Africa was by far the largest during the 1960-1995 period.

Before proceeding further with the discussion, we define some of the terms used above and others that occur in the literature. A **conflict** refers to "an interaction between interdependent people who perceive incompatible goals and who expect interference from the other party if they attempt to achieve their goal" (Draman, 2003). A **civil conflict** is a conflict between intra-state (as opposed to inter-state) parties. An **armed conflict** is a conflict featuring open combat with at least 25 battle related deaths per year (Draman, 2003). A **state-based armed conflict** is one "in which at least one of the warring parties is government of a state..." (HSRP, 2010) State-based armed conflicts featuring at least two states are termed **interstate conflicts**, while those involving the state government and at least one non-state armed group are termed **intrastate**, or **civil, conflicts.** Intrastate conflicts with armed forces from beyond the state's borders assisting one or more of the warring parties are classified as **internationalized intrastate conflicts**.

Civil War

Civil war has become the dominant form of war. A **civil war** is a civil conflict featuring open combat with at least 1000 battle- related deaths per year. Some researchers use the 1000 battle- related deaths as the threshold for civil war but as a cumulative figure rather than an annual requirement (Collier, 2000; Elbadawi and Sambanis, 2000). The 1000 battle-related deaths threshold (either annual or cumulative) is used as a proxy for the severity of the conflict. In recent discussions, conflicts featuring 1000 battle-related deaths are referred to as **high-intensity conflicts** (UNESCO, 2011).

Sambanis (2004) provides a detailed discussion of "coding rules" and their implications for separating a civil war from a civil armed conflict. Sambanis notes that the battle death rule ignores civilian deaths due to the conflict. He argues "civilians are targeted in civil war and are disproportionately affected by humanitarian disasters created by combatants to hold civilian populations hostage and gain control of territory." Recent discussions deal with battle-related deaths which includes battlefield combatants and civilians who die due to the effects of battle, directly or indirectly. Sambanis also argues that people who flee their homes out of fear for their lives also provide a measure of the human cost of the conflict. Sambanis proposes a classification for civil conflict versus civil war which has nine components. While very reasonable in terms of content, the definition has not have achieved broad usage. This is probably because it is much more complex than the simple battle- death rule.

Two additional descriptors for armed conflict refer not to the severity of the conflict but rather to the targets of the conflict. These include **"indiscriminant violence"** and **"one-sided violence"** (UNESCO, 2011). Indiscriminant violence is inflicted upon populations whether they include civilians or military combatants. With one-sided violence, civilians are the targets of the attacks.

Conflict-Affected Countries

Table 6 lists 35 **conflict-affected countries** identified by the Peace Research Institute Oslo (PRIO). In order to be included in the PRIO list the armed conflict must "entail contested incompatibility over government and/or territory where the use of armed force is involved, and where one of the parties to the conflict is the state." Furthermore, the countries include any which had battle-related deaths (military and civilian fatalities) exceeding 1000 during the 1999-2008 time period or more than 200 in any one year in 2006, 2007 or 2008.

Table 6: Conflict-Affected Countries, 1999-2008

Low Income countries	
SSA (12)	**Other Countries (4)**
Burundi*	Afghanistan*
CAR*	Myanmar
Chad*	Nepal*
Congo, DR*	Yemen*
Eritrea	
Ethiopia*	
Guinea*	
Liberia	
Rwanda	
Sierra Leone	
Somalia*	
Uganda*	
Lower Middle Income Countries	
SSA (4)	**Other Countries (10)**
Angola	Georgia*
Cote d'Ivoire	India*
Nigeria*	Indonesia
Sudan*	Iraq*
	Pakistan*
	OPT*
	Philippines*
	Sri Lanka*
	Thailand*
	Timor-Leste*
Upper Middle Income Countries	
SSA (None)	**Other Countries (5)**
	Algeria*
	Colombia*
	Russian Federation*
	Serbia
	Turkey*

Source: Modified from UNESCO (2011)
*Denotes current or recent conflict.

Of the 16 conflict-affected low income countries, 12 (75%) are from SSA. Of the 16 SSA conflict-affected countries, 12 (75%) are low-income countries. Slightly more than 25% of "other conflict-affected countries" are low-income countries.

Of the 35 conflict-affected countries in Table 6, only 25 (denoted by *) experienced a conflict during the 1999-2008 time interval. The other 10 are post-conflict but are considered to be at risk of another conflict.

Table 7: Number and Average Length of Conflict Episodes by Region, 1999-2008

Region	Number of conflicts 1999-2008	Average Length (Years)
SSA	20	9
Arab States	6	19
Central & Eastern Asia	3	14
Central Asia	1	17
East Asia & the Pacific	6	31
Latin America & The Caribbean	1	45
South & West Asia	11	24

Source: UNESCO (2011)

SSA has more conflicts (20) than other regions; however, the average length of SSA conflicts (9 years) is shorter than those of other regions. Table 8 shows the frequency and length of conflicts by income group.

Table 8: Number and Average Length of Conflict Episodes by Income Group, 1999-2008

Income Group	Number of conflicts 1999-2008	Average Length (Years)
Low Income	20	12
Lower Middle Income	23	22
Upper Middle Income	5	21

Source: UNESCO (2011)

As shown in Table 8, middle income countries had more conflicts and longer conflicts than the other income groups.

Causes of Civil War

Considerable research has been devoted to examining the causes of civil war. Drawing upon earlier work with his colleague, Anke Hoeffler, Collier (2000) uses a data set covering 161 countries for the period 1965-1999. During this time period there were 73 civil wars. Some of the war - countries lacked sufficient data for a complete analysis and needed to be dropped, leaving 47 civil wars in the set.

Countries with a high proportion of exports in their GDP were at elevated risk of civil war. An export/GDP rate of 25% was considered to be the threshold. Countries which have experienced a prior civil war were at more risk of another war and could be caught in a **conflict trap.** In such a trap the countries enter a cycle in which a conflict is followed by a breathing period which in turn is followed by another civil war.

Countries with large émigré populations residing in the US have a further elevated risk. Countries with little education are more likely to experience civil war. Countries in economic decline or with rapid population growth have elevated risk.

Overall, the risk of civil war was reduced following the end of the Cold War. Interestingly, and contrary to popular perceptions, increases in ethnic or religious diversity reduce the risk of civil war within countries. The exception to this diversity result occurs for countries where there is a dominant ethnic group. Collier defines **ethnic dominance** as a situation for which one ethnic group represents 45%-90% of the total population.

Income and wealth inequality have no impact on the risk of civil war, nor did a lack of democratic rights. These observations along with the inverse relationship between ethnic and religious diversity (except for countries with a dominant ethnic group) led Collier to conclude that objective "grievance" was not a cause of civil war.

Noting the positive relationship between the risk of civil war and the ratio of primary product exports to GDP, Collier concluded that "greed" rather than grievance is the underlying cause of civil wars. Primary commodities become targets of **predatory behavior** defined as the "the use of force to extort goods or money from their legitimate owners." Successful predation not only lines the pockets of the predators, it may also provide funding for their side of the conflict.

Nafziger and Auvinen (2002) use Gini data (not available to Collier) to measure income inequality, and counter to the findings of Collier, they found a relationship between civil war and inequality. They conclude, again counter to Collier, that "objective grievances of poverty and inequality contribute to war and humanitarian emergencies." They also found that education and employment differences, resource allocations and language discrimination contribute to conflicts. Their work does support Collier's findings that 1) natural resource products are an important source of conflict and 2) ethnicity is not a source of conflict. In earlier work they found a positive relationship between the ratio of military expenditures to national income.

Collier and Hoeffler (2000) use their global model of civil war over the 1965-1999 time- period to assess the causes of civil war in Africa (defined as SSA minus South Africa). First, they verified that the global model provided a good fit for Africa. They find that Africa has seen an increase in the incidence of civil war while non-African developing countries have seen a reduced incidence of civil wars over time. These divergent paths are explained by the differential economic performance of the two groups over the time period.

While Africa is more diverse than other developing countries, only 40% of African countries exhibit Collier's ethnic dominance compared to 57% in non-African developing countries which, other things being equal, should reduce the incidence of African civil wars relative to non-African countries. The Elbadawi and Sambanis results confirm the importance of income levels, the rate of growth of income, and the exports of primary products in causing civil war in Africa. Contrary to Collier's and Hoeffler's results, Elbadawi and Sambanis found another cause of civil war to be the lack of strong democratic institutions.

REFERENCES

Ayittey, G.B.N. 2010. The Worst of the Worst: Bad Dude Dictators and General Coconut Heads. *Foreign Policy.* July/August 2010, 90-91.

Collier, P. 2000. Economic Consequences of Civil Conflict and Their Implications for Policy. World Bank Manuscript.

Collier, P. and Hoeffler, A. 2000. On the Incidence of Civil War in Africa. World Bank Manuscript. www.worldbank.org/research/conflict/papers/incidence.htm

Commission for Africa (the Blair Commission Report). 2005. *Our Common Interest,* London.

Dickenson, E. 2010. Watch List: Four Countries in Big Trouble. *Foreign Policy.* July/August, 2010, 84-85.

Draman, R. 2003, Poverty and Conflict in Africa: Explaining a Complex Relationship. paper prepared for the Experts Group Meeting on Africa-Canada Parliamentary Strengthening Program, Addis Ababa, May, 2003.

Elbadawi, I. and Sambanis, N. 2000. Why Are There So Many Civil Wars in Africa? Understanding and Preventing Violent Conflict. *Journal of African Studies*. (9). 244-269.

Foreign Policy and the Fund for Peace. 2008. The Failed States Index. *Foreign Policy*. www.foreignpolicy.com

Foreign Policy and the Fund for Peace. 2010. The Failed States Index. *Foreign Policy.* July/August 2010. 76

Foreign Policy and the Fund for Peace. 2011. The Failed States Index. *Foreign Policy.* July/August, 48-49

Human Security Report Project (HSRP). 2010. The Causes of Peace and the Shrinking Cost of War. Vancouver, BC

Mo Ibrahim Foundation. 2008 Ibrahim Index of African Governance. www.moibrahimfoundation.org

Mo Ibrahim Foundation. 2010 Ibrahim Index of African Governance.

www.moibrahimfoundation.org

Mo Ibrahim Foundation. 2011 Ibrahim Index of African Governance. www.moibrahimfoundation.org

Mwachiro, K. 2010. Kenya corruption costs government dearly. BBC NEWS, December 3. www.bbc.co.uk/news/world-Africa. Retrieved 12-4-2010.

Nafziger, E. and Auvinen, A. 2002. Economic Development, Inequality, War, and State Violence. *World Development.* (30)2, 153-163.

OECD. 2008. Concepts and Dilemmas of State Building in Fragile Situations: From Fragility to Resilience.

Rice, S. and Patrick, S. 2008. Index of State Weakness in the Developing World. Brookings Institution.

Rotberg, R. 2002. Failed States in a World of Terror. *Foreign Affairs*. July-August, (81)4, 127-140.

Sambanis, N. 2004. What is Civil War? *Journal of Conflict Resolution.* December. Vol. 48 No. 6, 814-858.

Transparency International. 2009. Corruptions Perceptions Index 2009. www.transparency.org.

Transparency International. 2010. Corruptions Perceptions Index 2010. www.transparency.org.

Transparency International. 2011. Corruptions Perceptions Index 2011. www.transparency.org.

UN Development Program (UNDP). 2003. Millennium Development Goals: A compact among nations to end poverty. *Human Development Report (HDR) 2003.* New York, N.Y.

UN Millennium Project. 2005. (the Sachs Report). Investing in Development: A Practical Plan to Achieve the Millennium Development Goals. New York.

UNESCO. 2011. The Hidden Crisis: Armed conflict and education. *Education for All: Global Monitoring Report.*

World Bank. 2007. Confronting the Challenge of Gender Equality and Fragile States. *Global Monitoring Report 2007.* Washington D.C.

World Bank. 2009. *Atlas of Global Development*. Washington D.C.

World Bank. 2011. Silent and lethal: How quiet corruption undermines Africa's development efforts. *African Development Indicators, 2010.*

CHAPTER 6
FORCED MIGRATION AND DISPLACED PERSONS

Displaced persons do not sleep peacefully in their own beds because rough men stand ready to do violence to them

--With apologies to George Orwell[1]

The 2009 Global Monitoring Report noted that the countries making the most sluggish progress towards meeting the Millennium Development Goals are those fragile and conflict-affected states. More than half of these countries are in Sub- Saharan Africa. Collier (2007), in *The Bottom Billion,* commented that 73% of those people living in the bottom billion of people globally have been through a civil war or are still engaged in one. Collier refers to civil war as [economic] development in reverse. In discussing the costs of war, Collier points out that many people who die in civil war are not combatants killed in battle but rather civilian and other non-combatants who succumb to disease. Each year, around the world, several millions of people are forced to leave their homes involuntarily and join the ranks of individuals known collectively as displaced persons (DPs).

CATEGORIES OF DISPLACED PERSONS

First, we consider two broad categories of DPs. Persons who leave their homes and enter foreign countries are termed "refugees." Those persons who are displaced but remain within their own home- countries are termed "internally displaced persons" (IDPs).

We consider two sub-categories of refugees: those under the mandate of the United Nations High Commissioner for Refugees (UNHCR refugees); and Palestine Refugees who come under the mandate of the UN Relief and Works Agency for Palestine Refugees in the Near East (UNRWA refugees). These refugees are known as "statutory" refugees since they are covered by UN statutes. There are others who are refugees in name but do meet the definition of one or other of the two UN statutes. Consequently, they do not qualify for the protections provided by the UNHCR or the UNRWA conventions (discussed in Chapter 7).

Table 1 outlines the numbers of UN-recognized DPs and their composition from 2000 to 2010.

Table 1: The Number of UN Refugees, and IDPs, 2001-2010 (in millions of persons)

Year	2001	2002	2003	2004	2005	2006	2007	2008	2009	2010
Number of UNHCR Refugees	12.0	10.6	9.6	9.2	8.4	9.9	11.4	10.5	10.4	10.6
Number of UNRWA Refugees	3.8	---	---	4.0	4.3	4.3	4.6	4.7	4.8	4.7
Total Number of UN-Refugees	15.8	---	---	13.2	12.7	14.2	16.0	15.2	15.2	15.3
Number of IDPs of Concern to the UNHCR	1.2	----	4.2	5.4	6.6	12.8	13.7	14.4	15.6	14.7

Sources: UNHCR (2002, 2004, 2005, 2006, 2007b, 2008, 2009a, 2010, 2011), UNRWA (2011a)

The 1951 Convention relating to the status of refugees, modified by the 1967 Protocol (hereafter referred to as the 1951 Convention), formally defines a refugee (for the purpose of UNHCR assistance and support) as a person who:

> owing to well-founded fear of being persecuted for reasons of race, religion, nationality, membership of a particular social group or political opinion, is outside the country of his nationality and is unable or, owing to such fear, is unwilling to avail himself of the protection of that country; or who, not having a nationality and being outside the country of his former habitual residence is unable or, owing to such fear, is unwilling to return to it. (UNGA, 1951, 1967)

The number of UNHCR refugees decreased from 12 million persons in 2000 and 2001 to 8.4 million persons at the end of 2005. The trend reversed, briefly, in 2006 with an increase in refugees to 9.9 million persons by the end of the year. At the end of 2007, the number had increased to 11.4 million persons. The number of UNHCR refugees dropped to 10.5 million in 2008, to 10.4 million in 2009 and then increased in 2010 to 10.6 million persons—equal to the number of refugees in 2002. Over the period of 2001 to 2010, the number of refugees decreased by almost 1.4 million people. By contrast, the number of refugees increased dramatically during the earlier period of 1975 to 1993 increasing from 2.4 million in 1975 to 18.2 million in 1993.

Most UN-refugees (about two-thirds) are covered by the 1951 Convention; however, Palestine refugees are covered by the UN Relief and Works Agency for Palestine Refugees in the Near East (UNRWA). Under the UNRWA's original mandate, Palestine refugees are:

> people whose normal place of residence was Palestine between June 1946 and May 1948 who lost both their homes and livelihood as a result of the 1948 Arab-Israeli conflict. (UNRWA, 2011a)

The number of UNRWA refugees increased slowly but steadily over the past decade by one million persons over the years 2001 to 2009, and then dipped by 0.1 million in 2010. The total number of refugees, globally, declined by 0.5 million from 2001to 2010.

IDPs (of concern to the UNHCR) are defined as:

> Persons or groups of persons who have been forced or obliged to flee or to leave their homes or places of habitual residence, in particular as a result of or in order to avoid the effects of armed conflict, situations of generalized violence, violations of human rights or natural or human-made disasters, and who have not crossed an internationally recognized State border. (OHCHR, 1998)

The number of IDPs of concern to the UNHCR, in Table 1, includes only those persons displaced due to conflict situations. These IDPs have shown dramatic growth from 1.2 million in 2001 to 14.7 million in 2010. In 2009, the number of conflict-induced IDPs was slightly larger than the total number of refugees covered by the two UN mandates for the first time. In 2010, the number of IDPs (14.7 million) dropped below the total number of refugees (15.4 million) again.

Refugees

Originating and Host Country Profiles of Refugees

Table 2 presents the number of UNHCR refugees in the UNHCR regional classification for 2010. The three largest regions for refugees are Asia and Pacific (38%), Sub-Saharan Africa (21%) and the Middle East and North Africa (18%). The total number of UNHCR refugees was almost 10.6 million.

Table 2: Regional Distribution of UNHCR Refugees, 2010

UNHCR Region	Total Refugees End of 2010	%
Sub-Saharan Africa	**2,184,000**	**21**
Americas	804,000	8
Asia and Pacific	4,014,100	38
Europe	1,606,600	15
Middle East and North Africa	1,941,000	18
Overall Total	**10,549,700**	**100**

Source: UNHCR (2011)

Table 3 presents the 2010 distribution of UNRWA refugees across the five areas of its operations. Collectively, Gaza and the West Bank are referred to as the Occupied Palestinian Territory (OPT). Jordan hosted 2.0 million refugees, or 42.5% of the total, and the OPT countries hosted 1.9 million refugees, or 40% of the total. Syria and Lebanon hosted the remaining 0.9 million, or 19%.

Table 3: UNRWA Refugees by Host Country/Region, 2010

Region/Country	Number of Refugees (in millions)	% of Total	Number of Camps	Average Number Per Camp
Jordan	2.0	42.5	10	200,000
Gaza	1.1	23.4	8	137,500
West Bank	0.7	15	19	36,247
Syria	0.5	10.6	12*	41,333
Lebanon	0.4	8.5	12	37,017
Total	**4.7**	**100**	**61**	**77,049**

Source: Compiled from UNRWA (2011b)
Data as of December 31, 2010
* Includes 3 unofficial camps

The region has a total of 61 camps with an average of 77,049 refugees per camp. The average per camp varies widely between countries with the most densely populated being Jordan and the least dense being Lebanon.

Table 4: Seven Largest Countries of Origin for UNHCR Refugees, 2002 and 2010

Country of Origin For Refugees	Number of Refugees (in millions) 2010	Number of Refugees (in millions) 2002
Afghanistan	3.1	2.5
Iraq	1.7	0.4
Somalia	0.8	0.4
D.R. Congo	0.5	0.4
Myanmar	0.4	---
Sudan	0.4	0.5
Columbia	0.4	---
Burundi	---	0.6
Angola	---	0.4

Source: UNHCR (2011), Castles (2004)

Table 4 shows that, for both 2002 and 2010, Afghanistan was the largest originator of refugees. In 2010, Afghanistan contributed roughly 30% of global refugees. Roughly 96 percent of Afghan refugees settle in just two countries, Pakistan and Iran, both of which border Afghanistan. The second largest source country for refugees in 2010 is Iraq, and these refugees locate predominantly in Syria. Together, Afghanistan and Iraq account for 45% of UNHCR refugees globally. Somalia was the third largest source of refugees in 2010. Most Somali refugees settle in Ethiopia or Kenya. Afghanistan, Iraq and Somalia demonstrate the general result that most refugees stay close to their home countries. About 75% of refugees locate in neighboring countries or in other countries within their region (UNHCR, 2011). Colombia was one of the seven largest countries of origin in 2010, but not in 2002, and Burundi and Angola were on the 2002 top seven list but not on the 2010 list.

The 10 countries from Table 5 for 2010 account for roughly 62% of hosted-refugees covered by the UNHCR mandate. The country hosting the largest number of refugees is Pakistan in both years; however, the 2010 figure was 0.1 million persons smaller than in 2000. Only half of the countries on the 2010 top ten list were also on the list in 2000: Pakistan, Iran, Germany, China, and the United States.

Table 5: Ten Largest Host Countries for UNHCR Refugees, 2000 and 2010

Host Country	Number 2010 (in millions)	Number 2000 (in millions)
Pakistan	1.9	2.0
Syrian Arab Rep.	1.0	----
Islamic Rep. of Iran	1.1	1.9
Germany	0.6	0.9
Jordan	0.5	----
Kenya	0.4	---
Tanzania	---	0.7
Chad	0.4	---
China	0.3	0.3
United States	0.3	0.5
United Kingdom	0.2	---
FR Yugoslavia	---	0.5
Guinea	---	0.4
Sudan	---	0.4
DR Congo	---	0.3

Source: UNHCR (2011), Castles (2004)

Returning and Resettling Refugees

Offsetting the new refugees in 2010 were those refugees who voluntarily departed their country of refuge to return home or to be resettled in other countries. The countries to which the largest number of refugees returned are given in Table 6.

Table 6: Countries with the Largest Number of Returning Refugees, 2010

Country	Number of refugee returnees (thousands)
Afghanistan	118
Iraq	28.9
DR Congo	16.6
Rwanda	10.9
Sudan	7.1
Sri Lanka	5.1

Source: UNHCR (2011)

In 2010, 197,600 refugees returned to their countries of origin. Over half of these returned to Afghanistan.

As an alternative to returning to their home countries, refugees may voluntarily resettle in other countries. A total of 98,800 refugees were resettled in 22 countries in 2010. The 2010 resettlement numbers by country are given in Table 7 for six major resettlement countries.

Table 7: Six Major Resettlement Countries along with Their Respective Numbers and Percentages of Resettling Refugees

Country	Resettling refugees (thousands)	Percentage of Total
USA	71.4	72.2
Canada	12.1	12.3
Australia	8.5	8.6
Germany	2.0	2.0
Sweden	1.8	1.8
Norway	1.1	1.1

Source: UNHCR (2011)

The USA, Canada and Australia account for 93% of resettling refugees.

Table 8 shows the main countries from which refugees departed in 2010.

Table 8: Countries with the Largest Number of Refugee Departures or Voluntary Repatriation, 2010

Country	Number of refugee departures
Pakistan	109,400
DRC	14,500
Iran	10,200

Source: UNHCR (2011)

By far, Pakistan has the largest number of departures.

In 2010, seventy-three thousand resettling refugees received UNHCR-assistance. The main host countries of those receiving UNHCR-assistance are given in Table 9.

Table 9: Countries from Which Resettling Refugees Receiving UNHCR Assistance Departed, 2010

Refugees' home country	Number of UNHCR-assisted resettling refugees
Nepal	14,800
Thailand	11,400
Malaysia	8,000
Syria	7,200
Turkey	5,300

Source: UNHCR (2011)

The top three countries are in Asia with Nepal having the largest number.

Asylum-Seekers

Asylum-seekers are defined as "individuals who have sought international protection and whose claims for refugee status have not yet been determined." (UNHCR, 2010) The time profile of asylum-seekers and the number of countries receiving applications from 2004 to 2010 are given in Table 10.

Table 10: The Number of Asylum-Seekers and Application-Receiving Countries

Year	2004	2005	2006	2007	2008	2009	2010
# of First Instance Applications or Appeals (1000s)	680	668	596	653.8	875.3	948.4	845.6
# of Countries in which Applications were Submitted	143	149	151	154	154	159	166

Sources: UNHCR annual Global Trends Reports, 2005-2011

Location of Refugees: Camps versus Urban Areas

Paralleling demographic trends in the general population, refugees are becoming increasingly urbanized with about 50% of the 10.5 million UNHCR refugees in 2008 living in cities and towns. Major refugee cities include Abidjan, Amman, Bangkok, Bogota, Cairo, Damascus, Juba, Johannesburg, Khartoum, Nairobi, and Quito. Khartoum has 1.75 million refugees itself, and Bogota and Abidjan each have about one-half million DPs (UNHCR, 2009b). In 2009, the proportion of refugees living in urban areas increased to 58% (UNHCR, 2010b). Iran, Jordan, Pakistan, and Syria accounted for about 85% of urban refugees. In 2009, 58% of

UNHCR refugees were located in urban settings (UNHCR, 2010b). Two-thirds of the 4.7 million UNRWA refugees live in cities, towns and villages, while the remaining one-third of the refugees were located in camps or centers (UNRWA, 2011a).

Internally Displaced Persons (IDPs)

The protection situation for IDPs is quite different from refugees. There is no single international agency with a mandate to champion the cause of the IDPs. Over the years the UNHCR was called upon to provide assistance with IDPs given the expertise it had gained in working with refugees. The IDP situation has improved somewhat with the development of the "1998 Guiding Principles on Internal Displacement," by the 2004 creation of the position of Representative of the Secretary-General on the Human rights of Internally Displaced Persons and by the 2005 adoption of "the Cluster Approach" which coordinated the efforts of various agencies assisting IDPs.

Under the Cluster approach, the UNHCR is the lead agency, and it assumes responsibility for the establishment and management of camp facilities for IDPs. IDMC (2009) found that, in at least 26 countries, IDPs still faced violence in their area of refuge. The rationale offered for the absence of an international organization supporting IDPs is the principle of sovereignty which vests the responsibility for protecting IDPs in their respective domestic governments. However, this rationale falls apart when the government and its armed forces are the perpetrators of the abuse including the killing of IDPs.

While there is no global convention defining the rights of IDPs, Africa has developed regional versions. The most recent one is the African Union's Convention for the Protection and Assistance of Internally Displaced Persons in Africa (also known as the Kampala Convention). The Kampala Convention, approved in 2009, will only come into force when it has been ratified by at least 15 countries. At the end of 2010, only four countries (CAR, Chad, Sierra Leone, and Uganda) had ratified the Convention.

Persons covered by the 1951 Convention, the Cluster Approach for IDPs, and others receiving UNHCR assistance are termed "persons of concern" to the UNHCR.

Table 11 presents the major distribution of IDPs by region.

Table 11: Major Regions for IDPs, 2010

Region	IDPs (millions)	%
Africa (including North Africa)	11.1	40
Americas	5.4	20
South and South-East Asia	4.6	17
Middle East	3.9	14
Europe and Central Asia	2.5	9
Total	27.5	100

Source: IDMC (2011)

The 11.1 million IDP figure was a low point for Africa; however, Africa still accounted for 40% of estimated IDP populations in 2010. Over 40% of African IDPs in 2010 are located in Sudan.

Table 12 presents an historical comparison of the countries with the largest number of IDPs in 2003 and 2010.

Table 12: Countries with the Largest Number of IDPs 2003 and 2010

Country	IDPs 2010 (millions)	IDPs 2003 (millions)
Sudan	4.5-5.2	4.0
Colombia	3.6-5.2	2.9
Iraq	About 2.8	1.1
DRC	About 1.9	3.0
Somalia	About 1.5	---
Pakistan	About 1.0	---
Uganda	---	1.2

Source: IDMC (2011), Castles (2004)

In 2010, four of the seven countries in Table 12 are in Sub-Saharan Africa: Sudan, DRC and Somalia. In 2003, Uganda accounted for a large IDP population, but was replaced by Somalia and Pakistan in 2010.

Table 13 gives the regional distribution of new internal displacements in 2010.

Table 13: The Regional Distribution of New Internal Displacements, 2010

Region	Number (thousands)	%
Africa	1,230	42.4
South & South-East Asia	794	27.4
Americas	395	13.6
Europe and Central Asia	300	10.3
Middle East	177	6.1
Estimated total	2,900	100

Source: IDMC (2011)

Africa had the largest share of new IDPs at 42.4%. Together Africa and South and South-East Asia accounted for 70% of the total.

Table 14 shows the distribution of new IDPs across the ten largest countries.

Table 14: Countries with the Largest Number of New IDPs, 2009

Country	No. of New IDPs (thousands)
Sudan	495
Pakistan	400
DRC	400
Philippines	400
Somalia	300
Kyrgyzstan	300
Colombia	280
Sri Lanka	<300
Ethiopia	200
Yemen	200

Source: IDMC (2011)

Sudan had the largest new displacements. Four of the 10 countries in Table 14 are in SSA. These four SSA countries (DRC, Sudan, Somalia and Ethiopia) collectively accounted for 1.4 million new IDPs in 2010.

Returning IDPs

Reducing the stock of IDPs are those IDPs who returned to their homes from elsewhere within their country.

2010 saw more than two million IDPs return to their homes. Table 15 gives the numbers for six countries with the largest number of returnees. Three of the six are SSA countries (DRC, Uganda and Sudan), and these three accounted for 891,000 of the 2 million plus IDPs who returned to their respective home areas.

Table 15: Countries Having the Largest Reported Number of IDP Returnees, 2010

Country	Number of Returnees (thousands)
DRC	500
Pakistan	400
Uganda	271
Kyrgyzstan	225
Sri Lanka	150
Sudan	120

Source: IDMC (2011)

AGE AND GENDER COMPOSITION OF DPS

Table 16 presents the age-gender distribution of DPs in 2008.

Table 16: Age/Gender Distribution of DPs

	Females %						Males %					
	0-4	5-11	12-17	18-59	60+	Total	0-4	5-11	12-17	18-59	60+	Total
Refugees/ Asylum - Seekers	5	9	7	24	2	47	5	10	8	27	2	52
IDPs	5	9	7	26	3	50	3	5	10	7	26	51
Returned Refugees	9	12	7	19	2	49	9	13	8	19	2	51
Returned IDPs	11	13	6	25	1	56	1	10	10	6	17	44

Source: UNHCR (2009)

Not surprisingly, the 18-59 year old age group dominates all categories other than for IDPs. The largest group of females is found in the Returned IDP group. The smallest group of females is in the Refugee/Asylum – Seekers.

STATELESS PERSONS

Stateless persons are defined as "individuals not considered as citizens of any State under national laws" (UNHCR, 2010).

Table 17 gives the time profile of stateless persons reported by countries, the number of countries reporting them, and global estimates of stateless persons from 2004 to 2010.

According to Akram (2003), over one-half of Palestinians were stateless, and they formed the largest population of stateless persons in the world at that time.

Stateless persons are covered by the Convention relating to the Status of Stateless Persons, 1954 (OHCHR, 1996-2007), and the Convention on the Reduction of Statelessness, 1961 (UN, 2005).

Table 17: Stateless Persons Reported by Countries, the Number of Countries Reporting Stateless Persons, and Global Estimates of Stateless Persons

Year	2004	2005	2006	2007	2008	2009	2010
Countries Reporting	30	48	49	54	58	60	65
No. Reported By Countries (million)	1.5	2.4	5.8	3.0	6.6	6.6	3.5
Global Estimate (million)	11	11	15	12	12	12	12

Source: UNHCR Annual Reports, 2005-2011

ENDNOTE

1. Orwell's comment was affirmative: "Men sleep peacefully in their beds at night since rough men stand ready to do violence on their behalf."

REFERENCES

Akram, S. 2003. Stateless limbo, Al-Ahram Weekly. August 21-27, issue 652.

Castles, S. 2004. Confronting the Realities of Forced Migration. *Migration Information Source.* www.migrationinformation.org

Collier, P. 2007. *The Bottom Billion.* Oxford University Press. New York, NY.

Internal Displacement Monitoring Center (IDMC). 2009. Internal Displacement: Global Overview of Trends and Development in 2008.

Internal Displacement Monitoring Center (IDMC). 2011. Internal Displacement: Global Overview of Trends and Development in 2010.

Office of the United Nations High Commissioner for Human Rights (OHCHR). 1996-2007. Convention relating to the Status of Stateless Persons. 1954. www2.ohchr.org/English/law/stateless.htm

Office of the United Nations High Commissioner for Human Rights (OHCHR). 1998. Guiding Principles on Internal Displacement. www.unhchr.ch/html/menu2/7/b/principles.htm

United Nations (UN). 2005. Convention on the Reduction of Statelessness.1961.

United Nations General Assembly (UNGA). 1951. United Nations Convention Relating to the Status of Refugees.

United Nations General Assembly (UNGA). 1967. Protocol Relating to the Status of Refugees.

United Nations High Commissioner for Refugees (UNHCR). 2002. UNHCR releases 2001 global refugee statistics. Press Releases, June 18, 2002.

United Nations High Commissioner for Refugees (UNHCR). 2004. UNHCR: Sharp decline in refugees, others of concern in 2003. Press Releases, June 17, 2004.

United Nations High Commissioner for Refugees (UNHCR). 2005. 2004 Global refugee trends.

United Nations High Commissioner for Refugees (UNHCR). 2006. 2005 Global refugee trends.

United Nations High Commissioner for Refugees (UNHCR). 2007. 2006 Global Trends:refugees, asylum seekers, returnees, internally displaced and stateless persons.

United Nations High Commissioner for Refugees (UNHCR). 2008. 2007 Global trends:refugees, asylum seekers, returnees, internally displaced and stateless persons.

United Nations High Commissioner for Refugees (UNHCR). 2009a. 2008 Global trends:refugees, asylum seekers, returnees, internally displaced and stateless persons.

United Nations High Commissioner for Refugees (UNHCR). 2009b. Media Backgrounder: Responding to a growing challenge – protecting refugees in towns and cities. Media Page, December 7, 2009.

United Nations High Commissioner for Refugees (UNHCR). 2010a. 2009 Global trends:refugees, asylum seekers, returnees, internally displaced and stateless persons.

United Nations High Commissioner for Refugees (UNHCR). 2010b. Briefing notes, February 2, 2010.

United Nations High Commissioner for Refugees (UNHCR). 2010c. Briefing notes, February 12, 2010.

United Nations High Commissioner for Refugees (UNHCR). 2011. 2010 Global trends:refugees, asylum seekers, returnees, internally displaced and stateless persons.

United Nations Relief and Works Agency for Palestine Refugees in the Near East (UNRWA). 2007. The United Nations and Palestinian Refugees.

United Nations Relief and Works Agency for Palestine Refugees in the Near East (UNRWA). 2009. UNRWA Fact sheet.

United Nations Relief and Works Agency for Palestine Refugees in the Near East (UNRWA). 2011a. Palestine refugees: Who are Palestine refugees? UNRWA Web-Site, www.unrwa.org.

United Nations Relief and Works Agency for Palestine Refugees in the Near East (UNRWA). 2011b. Where we work. UNRWA Web-Site, www.unrwa.org.

CHAPTER 7
INTERNATIONAL HUMAN RIGHTS, INTERNATIONAL HUMANITARIAN LAWS, AND JUDICIAL BODIES

CLASSIFICATIONS OF LAWS

Treaty Law and Customary International Law

Treaty laws are written conventions establishing sets of rules by which consenting States agree to abide. Customary international laws are unwritten rules which are based upon 'general practices accepted as laws.' The rules and practices of customary international law apply to all States regardless of their own specific adherence to relevant treaties (ICRC, 2005a). ICRC (2005a) identified the following elements considered customary international humanitarian law:

Part I. The principle of distinction

Distinctions are made between civilians and combatants, civilian objects and military objectives, and the types of, and precautions regarding, attacks.

Part II. Specifically protected persons and objects

Includes Medical, Religious, Humanitarian Relief, and Peacekeeping Mission personnel and objects, and Journalists

Part III. Specific methods of warfare

Deals with Denial of Quarter, Destruction and Seizure of Property, Starvation and Access to Humanitarian Relief, Deception, and Communication with the Enemy

Part IV. Use of weapons

General Principles on the Use of Weapons, Poison, Biological Weapons, Chemical Weapons, Expanding Bullets, Exploding Bullets, Weapons Primarily Injuring by Non-detectable Fragments, Booby-Traps, Landmines, Incendiary Weapons, and Blinding Laser Weapons

Part V. Treatment of civilians and persons hors de combat

Fundamental Guarantees, Combatants and Prisoner-of-War Status, The Wounded, Sick and Shipwrecked, The Dead, Missing Persons, Persons Deprived of Their Liberty, Displacement and Displaced Persons, Other Persons Afforded Specific Protection

Part VI. Implementation

Compliance with International Humanitarian Law, Enforcement of International Humanitarian Law, Responsibility and Reparation, Individual Responsibility, War Crimes

International Humanitarian Law (IHL) and International Human Rights Law (IHRL)

International Humanitarian Law (IHL) and International Human Rights Law (IHRL) share objectives; however, they may apply under different situations. Both bodies of law seek 'to protect the lives and the health and dignity of individuals' (ICRC, 2003). IHL applies during times of armed conflict while IHRL applies in times of war and peace. The foundations of IHL are established in the 1949 Geneva Conventions I-IV and their associated Protocols. IHL is particularly concerned with the protection of civilian non-combatants in armed conflicts.

The basis of IHRL is found in the Conventions on Genocide, Racial Discrimination, Discrimination Against Women, and the Rights of the Child. In times of armed conflict both bodies of law apply in a complementary fashion (ICRC, undated). Since we are concerned here mainly with situations of intra-state armed conflict, we will consider both bodies of law together without distinction.

Many of the international humanitarian laws promulgated by the newly established United Nations in the late 1940s and early 1950s reflected the desire of the major nations to avoid a recurrence of the horrors committed in the lead up to and during WWII.

SOME KEY IHL AND IHRL CONVENTIONS/STATUTES

Oversight responsibility for the 1949 Geneva Conventions I-IV resides with the International Committee of the Red Cross (ICRC). The Geneva Conventions follow:

The 1949 Geneva Conventions I—IV

The four Conventions are:

- ***Convention (I) for the Amelioration of the Condition of the Wounded and Sick in Armed forces in the Field.***
- ***Convention (II) for the Amelioration of the Condition of the Wounded, Sick and Shipwrecked Members of Armed Forces at Sea.***
- ***Convention (III) relative to the Treatment of Prisoners of War.***
- ***Convention (IV) relative to the Protection of Civilian Persons in Time of* War.**

Conventions I—III are revisions of prior Geneva Conventions and deal with combatants, while Convention IV originated in 1949 and is the first to deal with protection of civilians during armed conflict. All four conventions have the same Article 3 which for the first time, deals with non-international (i.e. intrastate) armed conflicts. Article 3 also provides a set of prohibitions (Art. 3.1) including:

a) Violence to life and person, in particular murder of all kinds, mutilation, cruel treatment and torture
b) Taking of hostages
c) Outrages upon personal dignity, in particular humiliating and degrading treatment
d) The passing of sentences and the carrying out of executions without previous judgment pronounced by a regularly constituted court, affording all the judicial guarantees which are recognized as indispensable by civilized peoples.

Convention IV includes several articles calling for the specific protection of pregnant women, young children, and mothers with their children under the age of seven years old, recognizing their vulnerability.

While this Convention is not the first international document to emphasize the importance of protection of women, it is considered one of the most important in modern day humanitarian law. There are 194 state parties to the Conventions "making the Geneva Conventions universally applicable" (ICRC, 2009).

The Geneva Conventions have three "Additional Protocols." Additional Protocol I relates to Protection of Victims of International Armed Conflicts (ICRC, 1977a), and Additional Protocol II relates to the

Protection of Victims of Non-International Armed Conflicts (ICRC, 1977b). Additional Protocols I and II were promulgated in 1977. Additional Protocol III, added in 2005, deals with the Adoption of an Additional Distinctive Emblem (ICRC, 2009). Additional Protocol I, Article 77 and Additional Protocol II, Article 4.3, are devoted to the special and specific respect for, and protection of, children. Under additional Protocol II, Article 77, contracting states are responsible for preventing children under the age of fifteen years old from participating in any armed forces or conflict. Children, who have taken part in conflict while under age 15, are still protected by the Protocols. Detained children shall not be kept in the same quarters as detained adults. Any children under the age of eighteen shall not be subjected to the death penalty, despite the crime (ICRC, 1977b). Additional Protocol II, Article 4.3, states that children (a) shall be given access to education, (b) shall be given the effort of trying to reunite them with their families, (c) shall not be recruited into armed forces if under the age of 15 nor allowed to take part in hostilities, and (d) shall be relocated away from dangerous conflict zones by contracting states (ICRC, 1977b).

Prevention and Punishment of Genocide

The Convention on the Prevention and Punishment of the Crime of Genocide (UNGA, 1948)

Genocide, nearly always the result of identity-related conflicts, is one of the most heinous crimes on which humanity must unite to prevent and punish.

> --UN Secretary –General's Special Adviser on the Prevention of Genocide (OSAPG, 2009)

Article 2 of the Genocide Convention defines genocide as:

> "any of the following acts committed with intent to destroy, in whole or in part, a national, ethnical, racial or religious group:"
>
> (a) Killing members of the group;
> (b) Causing serious bodily or mental harm to members of the group;
> (c) Deliberately inflicting on the group conditions of life calculated to bring about its physical destruction in whole or in part;
> (d) Imposing measures intended to prevent births within the group; or

(e) Forcibly transferring children of the group to another group.

The historical basis for the Genocide Convention was the desire to avoid a repeat of the genocide known as the Holocaust in which 6 million Jews were killed at the hands of the Nazis during WWII.

Article 1 of the Convention states that "The Contracting Parties confirm that genocide, whether committed in time of peace, or in time of war, is a crime under international law which *they undertake to prevent and to punish*" (emphasis added). A total of 111 countries have joined the treaty as of March 24, 2010 which is a considerably lower number of signees than for some other treaties. However, the Office of the Special Adviser on the Prevention of Genocide (OSAPG) states that the Convention is part of international customary law and, as such, is considered to be applicable in all countries, even those who have not signed or ratified it (OSAPG, 2009). Furthermore, Article 1 "implies that national sovereignty cannot be invoked as a barrier to preventive involvement when genocide is or may be occurring" (OSAPG, 2009).

Prohibition of Torture

Article 3.1.a, which is common to each of the 1949 Geneva Conventions, lists cruel treatment and torture among the acts which "are and shall remain prohibited at any time and in any place whatsoever…"

Convention Against Torture and other Cruel, Inhuman or Degrading Treatment or Punishment, 1984 (CAT)

The CAT is the most detailed Convention concerning torture and other abuses.

Torture in the CAT is defined as:

> any act by which severe pain or suffering, whether physical or mental, is intentionally inflicted on a person for such purposes as obtaining from him or a third person information or a confession, punishing him for an act he or a third person has committed or is suspected of having committed, or intimidating or coercing him or a third person, or for any based on discrimination of any kind, when such pain or suffering is inflicted by or at the instigation of or with the consent or acquiescence of a public official or other person acting in an official capacity.

The CAT definition identifies physical and mental suffering as torture. Important characteristics necessary for an act to be classified as torture under the CAT include:

a) It must be inflicted purposely, and
b) It must be applied by or with the consent of a State official.

States parties to the CAT are expected to criminalize the use of torture. CAT places an absolute prohibition of the use of torture specifying that "No exceptional circumstance whatsoever, whether a state of war or a threat of war, internal political instability or any other public emergency, may be invoked as a justification of torture" (CAT, Art.1.2.2). CAT Art.3.1 also prohibits States party to Convention from expelling (the refoulement of) a person of another State whom is believed to be "in danger of being subjected to torture" as a result of the refoulement (CAT, Art. 3.1).

CAT provides for the prohibition of other cruel, inhuman or degrading treatment or punishment but falls short of requiring that such acts be criminalized (CAT, Art.16.1; Garcia, 2009). Garcia reports that 141 countries had signed the CAT by 2008.

The ***Optional Protocol to the Convention against Torture and other Cruel, Inhuman, or Degrading Treatment or Punishment*** **(UNGA, 2002)** deals mainly with administrative and procedural matters.

While torture, as defined by the CAT, is an act carried out by a public official, or with the acquiescence of one, with the intent of inflicting severe pain or suffering either physical or mental, these requirements are not universally invoked. In IHL the requirement of involvement by a public official is dropped and can be carried out by any individual (Reyes, 2007). The Inter-American Convention to Prevent and Punish Torture drops the "severe pain and suffering" requirement. Also, unlike the CAT's differential treatment of torture and "cruel, humiliating or degrading treatment," IHL treats them equally (Reyes, 2007).

The issue of "physical or mental" suffering raises the issue of physical versus psychological torture. Reyes (2007) points out that if it is difficult to adequately define torture in general, psychological torture is even more difficult. Since physical torture can cause both physical and mental suffering on its own, it is hard to specify a separate process for psychological torture. A breakthrough came from the Physicians for

Human Rights (PHR) in 2005. PHR based a definition of psychological torture on the United States Code of the prohibition of torture:

> Severe mental pain or suffering caused by the threat of, or actual, administration of procedures calculated to disrupt profoundly the senses or personality. (PHR, 2005)

This definition still requires the test for determining "severity." Reyes points out that it has been suggested that the suffering would need to be "prolonged," or "of substantial duration," "lasting months or even years." Post-traumatic stress disorder (PTSD) may qualify as an indicator of significant psychological harm having been inflicted. We will discuss PTSD later under violations of international laws.

Laws Protecting Women and Children

In civil wars, women and children always fare worst.

--*The Economist*. February 21, 2009, page 61.

It is generally known that women and children are especially vulnerable during armed conflicts, and even more so if they are internally displaced persons (IDPs). Accordingly, several laws have been issued to provide special protection to women and children beyond what is set forth in the Geneva Convention and protocol.

Protecting Women

Our focus below is on rape and sexual violence to women. The Fourth Geneva Convention provides for protection against rape. There is historical precedence leading to the protection. Experience in Asia during WWII provided the impetus for including such protection. In the infamous *Rape of Nanking* about 20,000 Chinese women were gang-raped and then killed by Japanese soldiers during the first month of Japanese occupation in 1937-38. This tragedy resulted in rape and sexual abuse being included in the Fourth Convention (HHI, 2010; *The History Place*, 2000). Specifically, Article 27 calls for the protection of women from attacks against "their honour, in particular against rape, enforced prostitution, or any form of indecent assault" (DCG, 1949d). Several articles specify that female internees (a) should be kept in separate chambers from male internees, (b) shall have the supervision of a female, (c) should be provided separate sanitation areas apart from those used by male internees, and (d) are to be searched only by females (DCG, 1949d).

Further rights for women are specified in the following:

- ***Declaration on the Elimination of Discrimination against Women (UNGA, 1967)***
- ***Convention on the Elimination of all Forms of Discrimination Against Women (UNGA, 1979)***
- ***Declaration on the Elimination of Violence Against Women (UNGA, 1993)***

Sexual assaults are covered in Articles 2(a) and 2(b) of the Declaration on the Elimination of Violence Against Women. These articles make it clear that both marital rape and rape occurring within the general community are encompassed. Only six members of the UN have not ratified the 1993 Declaration. These include: Iran, Palau, Somalia, Sudan, Tonga and the United States.

Protecting Children

Convention on the Rights of the Child (UNGA, 1989)

While there are additional documents which were written throughout the last century regarding the special needs of children, the Convention on the Rights of the Child (1989), along with its associated Optional Protocol (2000), address more modern issues of children's needs and their special protection (UNGA, 2008). The Child Rights Convention has been signed by 193 countries making it one of the most signed of the international humanitarian laws along with the Geneva Conventions.

Article 9 stipulates that no child shall be removed from his parents or family against his or her will. However, in the event that there is abuse or neglect by the child's parents or guardians, the State is expected to assist in protecting the child and to work towards relocation in the best interests on the child. Under this article, as well as those addressed in basic human rights documents, children have the right to live a life without abuse and inflicted harm even when those causing the harm may be the natural or legal caregivers to the child. Therefore, the State is responsible to take any reports of abuse from children as a serious offence and act within their means to provide the children with a safe alternative to avoid further abuse.

Articles 20-22 are of particular importance to the issue of orphaned or separated refugee children. In those articles, it is explained that in the case of a child without parents or guardians that the State must work towards finding an appropriate means of supervision such as a foster family or adoption. While this often does indeed occur within refugee camps as children are placed into foster families of their same ethnic or religious background as is emphasised in this document, the children are often abused by these foster or adoptive families. States are responsible for the protection of the child even after the placement in a foster family or an adoptive family.

Because of the additional stress surrounding issues of civil war, armed conflict, and refugee camps, it is understandable that there is little time and energy to be placed on following up on the placement of children but for the sake of the children and in the name of human rights and international law, there should be stronger emphasis on reinforcing the protection of vulnerable children. Especially important here is Article 22 which noted that there should be special cooperation between State parties, the United Nations, and non-governmental organisations in order to ensure the protection of children in this particular situation. Although there are additional factors surrounding the refugee camps and armed conflict in relation to the child, the State is encouraged to seek additional help if needed.

Article 27 states that children have the right to an adequate standard of living regarding their emotional, physical, mental, social lives, etc. Article 34 states that State parties are required to do everything within their capacity to protect children from any kind of sexual exploitation or abuse, and Article 36 says that the States must do everything they can in order to protect the children from all other forms of exploitation prejudicial to any aspects of the child's welfare. Article 38 says that States must strive to protect the children from being involved in hostilities, such as acting in conflict, and are responsible to ensure that the rights under international humanitarian law are respected and upheld during the time of armed conflict. In particular, states parties are to refrain from recruiting persons less than 15 years of age into the armed forces and to endeavour to ensure that no persons less than 15 years of age engage in hostilities.

It is often argued that the Convention for the Rights of the Child is one of the weakest treaties and one of the hardest to enforce. There are many reasons for this. One reason is that, being young, children have little knowledge. Also, in the regions of the world where child soldiers are heavily recruited, they are undereducated. If they are not told what legal rights they have, they cannot know those rights are being violated. They cannot report their abuse if they do not understand that it is illegal. Another reason is that children are often very naive and afraid of what may happen if they do tell someone about what has happened to them. Perpetrators use this to their utmost advantage by threatening to kill friends and family members if the children tell anyone about abuse. Finally, children are often easily influenced by others.

The Optional Protocol to the Convention on the Rights of the Child on the Involvement of Children in Armed Conflict (2000)

The major element in the Optional Protocol is the increase in the minimum age for persons engaged in armed conflict to at least18 years old. Also, the Protocol specifies that recruitment of persons under age 18 to the armed forces (in non-a non-combatant role) is not to be compulsory.

The Paris Principles (2007)

The most recent document dealing with the protection of children in armed conflict is *The Paris Principles* (UNICEF, 2007) which is based upon the 1997 *Capetown Principles* dealing with children and armed forces (UNICEF, 1997).

Laws Protecting Displaced Persons

Concern for Europeans displaced by World War II resulted in the United Nations General Assembly establishing the Office of the UNHCR effective 1950 and the 1951 United Nations Convention Relating to the Status of Refugees. This Convention specified UNHCR refugees as persons satisfying the definition by 1951, and it implicitly concerned only persons in Europe. The 1951 Convention was modified by the 1967 Protocol Relating to the Status of Refugees removing the time (1951) and geography (Europe) restrictions imposed in the original Convention. The 1951 Convention, modified by the 1967 Protocol, is referred to as the 1951 Convention.

While most UN-refugees (about two-thirds) are covered by the 1951 Convention, Palestine refugees are covered by the UN Relief and Works Agency for Palestine Refugees in the Near East (UNRWA) which was established in December 1949 following the 1948 Arab-Israeli war.

Internally displaced persons face two challenges for their protection. First, there is no single international agency to champion the cause of the IDPs. Second, there is no international convention stipulating the rights of

IDPs. The situation improved somewhat with the production of the 1998 Guiding Principles on Internal Displacement, the 2004 creation of the position of Representative of the Secretary-General on the Human rights of Internally Displaced Persons and the adoption of the Cluster Approach in 2005 whereby the UNHCR assumes some responsibility for IDPs.

NON-JUDICIAL AND JUDICIAL AUTHORITIES/ PROCESSES FOR INTERNATIONAL LAW

Non-Judicial Process: Truth Commissions

Truth Commissions investigate past history of conflict as part of the healing process. Hayner (2001) sets forth four major features of truth commissions. Truth commissions:

- are not ongoing bodies but rather focus on past event,
- investigate a pattern of abuse over a period of time rather than specific episodes. The mandate specifies the time period and the type of human rights violation to be examined,
- truth commissions are temporary, generally operating from 6 months to two years in many cases; however, some run over several years,
- truth commissions are empowered or sanctioned by the State.

Table 1 documents the SSA countries which had truth commissions between 1974 and 2004.

Countries with truth commissions post 2004 include; (2005) Liberia, (2008) Kenya, (2009) Togo (Amnesty International, 2010), and (2011) Cote d'Ivoire (BBC, 2011a).

Table 1: Truth Commissions in Sub-Saharan Africa, 1974-2004

Country	Commission Date	Time Period Covered
Uganda	1974	1971-74
Zimbabwe	1985	1983
Uganda	1986-1995	1962-86
Chad	1991-92	1982-90
Rwanda	1992-93	1990-92
Burundi	1995-96	1993-95
South Africa	1995-2000	1960-94

Nigeria	1991-2001	1966-99
Sierra Leone	2002	1991-99
Ghana	2002	1966-2001

Source: Brahm (2004)

The International Court of Justice

Chapter XIV, Article 92 of the UN Charter stipulates that "The International Court of Justice (ICJ) shall be the principle judicial organ of the United Nations." The ICJ, residing at the Hague in the Netherlands, deals only with nation- to- nation problems, and hence it does not deal with war crimes committed by individuals.

International Criminal Tribunals

The UN Charter Article 95 permits member countries to utilize other tribunals for resolving issues. These tribunals are part of a movement that began with the advent of the international military tribunals used in Nuremberg, Germany and in Tokyo, Japan following WWII (Kaye, 2011). During the 1990s, various International Criminal Tribunals were established for specific countries to deal with crimes committed by individuals within those specific countries during a specified period of time.

The ***International Criminal Tribunal for Rwanda (ICTR)*** was established in November 1994 "...for the prosecution of persons responsible for genocide and other serious violations of international humanitarian law committed in the territory of Rwanda between 1 January 1994 and 31 December 1994." In July/August 2010 Dominique Ntawukulilyayo, a former Rwanda official, was sentenced to 25 years in jail for his role in the Rwanda genocide. The split judgment rendered means that he could be acquitted on appeal. In total, the ICTR sentenced 46 defendants and acquitted eight. There are two dozen additional trials on the docket (Kaye, 2011).

In June 2011, ex-minister Pauline Nyiramasuhuko became the first woman convicted for genocide in Rwanda by the ICTR (BBC, 2011b). Along with her son, she was accused of organizing the kidnapping and rape of Tutsi women and girls. Nyiramasuhuko was sentenced to life in prison.

The UN-backed ***Special Court for Sierra Leone*** is charged with trying "those who bear the greatest responsibility for serious violations of international humanitarian law and Sierra Leonean law committed in the territory of Sierra Leone since 30 November 1996." The Prosecutor issued 13 indictments in 2003, two of which were withdrawn due to deaths of two alleged perpetrators. Trials for eight of the 11 have been completed. Former Liberian President, Charles Taylor's trial was in the Defense stage during the summer of 2010. He is accused of funding a former Sierra Leone rebel group, the Revolutionary United Front (RUF), by selling diamonds (known as blood diamonds) to purchase weapons. Taylor is charged with 11 cases of war crimes and crimes against humanity. These include five charges involving violations of Article 3 common to the four Geneva Conventions and/or Protocol II, another five involving crimes against humanity, and one charge of using child soldiers under 15 years of age (BBC NEWS, 2010c).

A tribunal for Kenya was to be established to deal with alleged perpetrators of the violence that lead to the deaths of some 1300 to 1500 people following the 2007 elections (BBC News, 2009 a, b). The tribunal was to be in place by July 2010. Kenya objected strenuously to the alleged perpetrators listed by the prosecution, and the government voted to withdraw from membership in the judicial body. Given the inability of the Kenyans to establish their own Tribunal, the International Criminal Court (see below) took over the process.

The Statute of Rome: The International Criminal Court (ICC)

Absent a permanent international judicial body to deal with such incidences, each new situation necessitates the establishment of a new tribunal specific to the situation under investigation. This tedious situation was remedied by the establishment of the International Criminal Court (ICC). Countries may opt for a trial through the ICC or establish their own tribunal with approval of the ICC.

In July 1998, 120 UN States adopted the Statute of Rome establishing the International Criminal Court as a permanent institution located at The Hague in the Netherlands. The Statute came into force on July 1, 2002, and at the end of 2010 the ICC had 114 member states (Kaye, 2011). The ICC's jurisdiction is limited to crimes committed after July 1, 2002, and it only deals with persons who are aged 18 or older at the time of the alleged crime. The overall mandate for the ICC is "to exercise its jurisdiction over persons for the most serious crimes of international concern…"

The "most serious crimes" include the following broad categories:

1) The crime of genocide
2) Crimes against humanity
3) War crimes, and
4) The crime of aggression.

The types of crimes for the first three broad categories are set forth in Articles 6, 7 and 8 of the Statute. The fourth category, crimes of aggression, was not defined due to a lack of agreement among members. No agreement regarding aggression has been reached as of the time of this writing; however, it was expected to be a major topic at the June 2010 meeting of the ICC.

As of December, 2011, seven countries are facing investigation: Cote d'Ivoire, Kenya, Libya, Central African Republic, the Democratic Republic of Congo, Sudan, and Uganda. The ICC investigations of Central African Republic, the D.R. Congo, and Uganda are being undertaken at the request of the respective countries. The Sudan case relates to Darfur and was referred to the ICC by the UN Security Council. Cote d'Ivoire's new President, Alassane Ouatarra, requested an ICC investigation of the violence following the 2010 election (*The Economist,* 2011). Former President Laurence Gbagbo faces four charges of crimes against humanity by the ICC in The Hague (BBC, 2011c). As noted above, Kenya was to establish a separate ITC; however, it failed to do so which resulted in the ICC to taking over. Libya is facing investigations following the violence during the uprising in 2011. The fact that all countries under investigation, with the exception of Libya, are from SSA has not been lost on those wanting to be critical of the ICC's actions.

REFERENCES

Amnesty International. 2010. Commissioning justice; truth commissions and criminal justice. London, U.K.

BBC NEWS (BBC). 2006. The Charges against Charles Taylor. 4-3-2006. News.bbc.co.uk. Retrieved 8-9-2010.

BBC NEWS (BBC). 2009a. Kenya sets new tribunal deadline. 7-4-2009. newsvote.bbc.co.uk. Retrieved 7-3-2009.

BBC NEWS (BBC). 2009b. ICC seeking speedy Kenya trials. 11-7-2009. newsvote.bbc.co.uk. Retrieved 11-7-2009.

BBC NEWS (BBC). 2011a. Ivory Coast gets truth and reconciliation commission. 9-28-2011. www.bbc.co.uk/news/world-africa . Retrieved on 9-30-2011.

BBC NEWS (BBC). 2011b. Rwanda: Ex-women's minister guilty of genocide, rape. 6-24-2011. www.bbc.co.uk/news/world-africa . Retrieved on 6-24-2011.

BBC NEWS (BBC). 2011c. Ivory Coast's Laurent Gbagbo appears at ICC in Hague. 12-5-2011. www.bbc.co.uk/news/world-africa . Retrieved on 12-5-2011.

Brahm, E. 2004. Truth Commissions. www.Beyondtractability.org . June.

Diplomatic Conference of Geneva (DCG), 1949a. Convention (I) for the amelioration of the condition of the wounded and sick in armed forces in the field. Geneva, 12 August 1949.

Diplomatic Conference of Geneva (DCG), 1949b. Convention (II) for the amelioration of the condition of the wounded, sick and shipwrecked members of armed forces at sea. Geneva, 12 August 1949.

Diplomatic Conference of Geneva (DCG), 1949c. Convention (III) relative to the treatment of prisoners of war. Geneva, 12 August 1949.

Diplomatic Conference of Geneva (DCG), 1949d. Convention (IV) relative to the protection of civilian persons in time of war. Geneva, 12 August 1949.

The Economist. 2009. Civilians in war zones: women and children fare worst. 2-21-2009, p. 61.

The Economist. 2011. The International Criminal Court bares its teeth. 5-14-2011. 57-58,

Garcia, M. J. 2009. UN Convention Against Torture (CAT): Overview and Application to Interrogation Techniques. Congressional Research Service. www.crs.gov.

Harvard Humanitarian Initiative (HHI) 2010. "Now, the world is without me": an investigation of sexual violence in eastern democratic republic of Congo. Harvard Humanitarian Initiative and Oxfam.

Hayner, P. B. 2001. *Unspeakable truths*. Routledge, N.Y.

The History Place. 2000. Genocide in the 29th century: the rape of Nanking 1937-1938. www.historyplace.com/worldhistory/genocide/nanking.htm.

International Committee of the Red Cross (ICRC). 1977a. Protocol Additional to the Geneva Conventions of 12 August 1949, and relating to the protection of victims of international armed conflicts (Protocol I). 8 June 1977.

International Committee of the Red Cross (ICRC). 1977b. Protocol Additional to the Geneva Conventions of 12 August 1949, and relating to the protection of victims of non-international armed conflicts (Protocol II). 8 June 1977.

International Committee of the Red Cross (ICRC). 2003. International Humanitarian Law and International Human Rights Law: Similarities and differences. www.ehl.icrc.org. Retrieved 11-1-2011

International Committee of the Red Cross (ICRC). 2005a. Study on customary international humanitarian law: a contribution to the understanding and respect for the rule of law in armed conflict.

International Committee of the Red Cross (ICRC). 2005b. Protocol Additional to the Geneva Conventions of 12 August 1949, and relating to the adoption of an additional distinctive emblem (Protocol III), 8 December 2005.

International Committee of the Red Cross (ICRC). 2009. The Geneva conventions of 1949. March 9, 2009. www.icrc.org. Retrieved 6-3-2010.

International Criminal Court (ICC) 2010. ICC at a glance. www.icc-cpi.int Retrieved 7-20-2010.

Kaye, D. 2011. Who's Afraid of the International Criminal Court? Finding the Prosecutor Who Can Set It Straight. *Foreign Affairs*. 90(3), 118-129.

Office of the Special Adviser on the Prevention of Genocide (OSAPG). 2009. Prevention of genocide. Booklet on what is genocide, why it happens and what is the role of the Special Adviser of the Secretary General, the United Nations system and the International Criminal Court. UN Department of Public Information / the Office of the Special Adviser on the Prevention of Genocide. February 2009. www.un.org/preventgenocide/adviser .

Physicians for Human Rights (PHR). 2005. *Break Them Down.* Report by Physicians for Human Rights, Washington, D.C.

Reyes, H. 2007. The worst scars are in the mind: psychological torture. *International Review of the Red Cross*. 89(867), 591-617.

The Straits Times. 2010. Rape capital of the world. April 28. www.straitstimes.com/Breaking News/World/Story/STIStory_519993.html. Retrieved 7-28-2010.

United Nations (UN). 2002. Rome Statute of the International Criminal Court.

United Nations General Assembly (UNGA). 1948. Convention on the prevention and punishment of the crime of genocide. www.unhchr.ch Retrieved on 5-17-2009.

United Nations General Assembly (UNGA). 1967. Declaration on eliminating discrimination against women.

United Nations General Assembly (UNGA). 1975. Convention Against Torture and Other Cruel, Inhuman or Degrading Treatment or Punishment. www.hrweb.org.

United Nations General Assembly (UNGA). 1979. Convention on the elimination of all forms of discrimination against women (known as CEDAW).

United Nations General Assembly (UNGA). 1989. Convention on the rights of the child.

United Nations General Assembly (UNGA). 1993. Declaration on eliminating violence against women. 85th Plenary Meeting.

United Nations General Assembly (UNGA). 2000. Optional protocol to the convention on the rights of the child on the involvement of children in armed conflict.

United Nations General Assembly (UNGA). 2002. Optional Protocol to the Convention Against Torture and Other Cruel, Inhuman or Degrading Treatment or Punishment.

United Nations High Commissioner for Refugees (UNHCR). 2010. UNHCR condemns endemic rape in DRC, helps survivors. www.unhcr.org/print/4bd18e7e9.html. Retrieved 7-29-2010.

UNICEF. 1997. The Capetown principles and best practices on the prevention of recruitment of children into the armed forces and on the demobilization and reintegration of child soldiers in Africa. April 1997.

UNICEF. 2007. The Paris principles: the principles and guidelines on children associated with armed forces or armed groups. February 2007

United Nations Relief and Works Agency for Palestine Refugees in the Near East (UNRWA). 2009. UNRWA Fact sheet. www.unrwa.org.

United Nations Security Council Report (UNSC). 2006. Protection of civilians in armed conflict. Update Report No. 5, June 21.

United Nations Security Council Report (UNSC). 2010a. Children in armed conflict: Report of the Secretary General.

United Nations Secretary Council (UNSC). 2010b. Children and armed conflict: Report of the Secretary-General.

CHAPTER 8
VIOLATIONS OF INTERNATIONAL LAWS: SELECTED EXAMPLES

In Chapter 7, we discussed the body of international law that has evolved to protect civilian non-combatants and displaced persons during periods of armed conflict. Unfortunately, these laws are ignored frequently. In this chapter we discuss examples of the violations of international law.

VIOLATIONS OF THE GENOCIDE CONVENTION

Far from being consigned to history, genocide and its ilk remain a serious threat. Not just vigilance but a willingness to act are as important today as ever.

> --Ban Ki-moon, on the occasion of the 60th Anniversary of the Genocide Convention (OSAPG, 2009)

Since 1990, Sub-Saharan Africa has experienced two episodes of genocide. The first episode occurred in Rwanda in 1994, and the second episode, in Darfur, Sudan in the mid-2000s.

Rwanda

> *This book [Shake Hands with the Devil] is a cri de Coeur (cry from the heart) for the slaughtered thousands, a tribute to the souls hacked apart by machetes because of their supposed difference from those who sought to hang onto power. It is the story of a commander who, faced with a challenge that didn't fit the classic Cold War-era peacekeeper's rule book, failed to find an effective solution and witnessed, as if in punishment, the loss of some of his own troops, the attempted annihilation of an ethnicity, the butchery of children barely out of the womb, the stacking of severed limbs like cordwood, the mounds of decomposing bodies being eaten by the sun.*
>
> --Lt. Gen. Romeo Daillaire and Maj. Brent Beardsley (2004)

As the passage by General Daillaire and Major Beardsley shows, the conflict in Rwanda was horrific. The use of genocide was universally acknowledged with shame being expressed by the international community at having allowed the massacre to continue. In early 1994, about 800,000 members of the Tutsi tribe and moderate Hutus were killed by the Hutu tribe. Some further insight into the horror of the in Rwanda genocide can be gleaned from the emotionally charged film *Hotel Rwanda*. The international community vowed that such an episode would never occur again.

Important results emerged from the deliberations of the International Criminal Tribunal for Rwanda (ICTR), along with Yugoslavia's ICTY. These tribunals recognized rape as a form of torture (Strumpen-Darrie, 2000). Furthermore, the ICTR recognized rape as a form of genocide (Strumpen-Darrie, 2000).

Darfur, Sudan

Darfur is today's capital of human suffering

> --Elie Wiesel. Foreword, 2007. Cheadle and Prendergast (2007)

Darfur is home to the first genocide of the twenty-first century. After the genocide in Rwanda, in which 800,000 people were killed, the world said we would not tolerate this ever again. Amazingly, the words "Never Again" have continued to be uttered in the months -- and now years—that have passed since 2003, when the killing started in the remote western region of Sudan. We continue to hear people say this genocide cannot continue, but it continues every day. Up to 400,000 have been killed and millions displaced.

> --Senators Barack Obama and Sam Brownback. Introduction. Cheadle and Prendergast (2007)

The conflict in Darfur is highly visible but wrapped in international controversy. The Darfur region is located in the western part of the Sudan and borders Chad. The peoples of Darfur consist of some 36 main tribes of which the three largest non-Arab groups are: the Fur, Masalit, and Zaghawa, with the Fur being the largest group in Darfur. (Darfur is composed of two words, Dar, meaning home and Fur referring to the people. Darfur, then, is the "home of the Fur" (Cheadle and Prendergast, 2007)). These Africans, of the Muslim faith, are the target of the Arab militia, the Janjaweed, in fighting that began in 2003. The Arab assault went beyond the rebel fighters to attacking civilians in a brutal fashion. An informative source for Darfur issues is Cheadle and Prendergast (2007).

In September, 2004 Secretary Colin Powell used the term genocide to describe the Darfur situation, and was followed by President George W. Bush stating that genocide was occurring in Darfur. In 2005, the UN Security Council referred the Darfur case to the ICC. In a high profile and contentious move, the ICC issued a warrant for the arrest of Sudan's President Omar al-Bashir over alleged atrocities in Darfur on March 4, 2009. The warrant lists two counts of war crimes and five counts of crimes against humanity. Originally the ICC warrant also included three counts of genocide; however, they were dropped when the Pre-Trial Chamber ruled against the evidence presented for genocide. Bashir and the Sudanese government have ignored the warrant saying they do not recognize the ICC's jurisdiction. Bashir is the first sitting head of government to be charged by the ICC. Very soon after the warrant was issued, Bashir received expressions of support from Libya and Egypt. The African Union issued a statement that it would not cooperate with the ICC (BBC NEWS, 2009a). The Arab League issued a similar statement (BBC NEWS, 2009b). These two groups called on the UN Security Council to suspend the case under Article 16 of the Rome Statute. Four of the five permanent members of the Security Council (Britain, China, France and Russia), expressed their support for the suspension! The various parties backing the suspension argued that the charges by the ICC would "hamper" the peace process. It has been more than a year that Bashir has ignored the warrant. Has there been progress on peace in the region? Nonetheless, Bashir's travels outside of Africa and the Middle East were blocked due to fear of arrest. Some people who reject the ICC decision or do not accept its jurisdiction have expressed various objections. Some "see the ICC as an attempt by the West to interfere in their affairs." (BBC NEWS, 2009a). The president of Malawi, Bingu wa Mutharika, complained that the ICC warrant for Bashir was "undermining African Solidarity and African peace and security." (BBC NEWS, 2009a) Syrian President Bashar al- Assad said that those "who had committed massacres and atrocities in Palestine, Iraq, and Lebanon should be arrested first" (BBC NEWS, 2009b).

The ICC "reported Sudan" to the UN Security Council for its refusal to arrest two other suspected war criminals, Ahmed Haroun and Ali Muhammad Al Abd-Rahman (BBC NEWS, 2010a). The ICC also filed an appeal against the pre-trial chamber's ruling against the original genocide charges. The Appeals Court reversed the pre-trial chamber's decision and the latter body was to reconsider its ruling. The pre-trial chamber then concurred with allowing the genocide charge to go forward. On July 12, 2010 the ICC issued a second warrant for Bashir's arrest.

This time the warrant had three counts of genocide. Bashir remains defiant.

PROTECTION OF WOMEN AND CHILDREN

Women and children are throw-away items all across Africa

--Cindy McCain, Morning Joe, MSNBC, March 10, 2010.

Violation of Women's Rights: Rape and Other Forms of Sexual Abuse

Rape is an extremely effective wartime weapon...By systematically raping women and girls, armed groups assert power and domination over not only the women but their men as well.

--Harvard Humanitarian Initiative, 2010.

Rape anytime, and anywhere, is a heinous crime against human dignity. Rape in Africa is a strategic weapon of war designed to terrorize individuals, families, communities, and entire groups (populations) of individuals. The Rome Statute (UN, 2002) includes "rape, sexual slavery, enforced prostitution, forced pregnancy, enforced sterilization, or any other form of sexual violence" against women as Crimes against humanity (Article 7, 1g) and as War crimes (Article 8, 2b.xxiii; and 2e.vi for "armed conflict not of an international character).

In 2010, Ms. Margot Wallstrom, a senior UN official, proclaimed the Democratic Republic of the Congo (DRC) (already known as the worst place in the world to be a woman or a child) to be the "Rape Capital of the World" (HRW, 2009; *The Straits Times*, 2010). Various documents note that "true" estimates of the incidence of sexual violence are not known (HHI, 2010). However, they do provide "estimates." HRW (2009) indicates that in the first nine months of 2009 more than 7,500 cases of sexual violence against females occurred in the eastern DRC provinces of North and South Kivu. A UNHCR spokeswoman, Melissa Fleming, reported that UN data shows that throughout the DRC 1,244 women were sexually assaulted during the first three months of 2010 (Schlein, 2010). The eastern provinces of North and South Kivu account for more than one third of the UN estimate. Fleming also reported that at least 200,000 cases of sexual violence in the DRC have been reported since 1996.

HHI (2010) conducted a survey of sexual violence survivors who had gone to Panzi Hospital in South Kivu between 2004 and 2008 and who requested assistance from the Victims of Sexual Violence Program. A total of 4,311 records were reviewed. The survey collected demographic information as well as allowing survivors to describe their experience. It is not clear how much the results generalise across other regions; however, the "picture" that emerges is very interesting. The age of victims ranged from 3.5 to 80 with an average age of 35. The majority of women (a) were married (53%), (b) were illiterate (59%), (c) were members of the Bashi tribe (65%), and (d) reported agriculture as the main source of livelihood (74%). Females taken as sex slaves were younger than those of other forms of violence, and they were more likely to be single. The majority of sexual violence perpetrators were identified as armed combatants (52%). A significant portion of those identified simply as "assailants" (42%) were thought to be armed combatants as well given the characteristics of the assault. The majority of assaults were gang rapes (60%). The time period witnessed an increase in civilians as rape perpetrators.

Disturbingly, soldiers from the government's own army were guilty of violating human rights and committing war crimes or crimes against humanity. Between January and September 2009, the Congolese soldiers and their coalition partner, the Rwandan Defence Force (RDF), were responsible for killing 732 civilians including 143 Rwandan Hutu refugees. The killings, done by the Congolese soldiers, also involved the rape of women and girls. Out of 410 sexual violence cases documented by HRW, 268 were by Congolese soldiers (HRW, 2009). Gambino (2008) in his brief report on the Congo writes "The army and police are not only unable to maintain order in the eastern provinces, they are also part of the problem, each regularly committing horrible abuses against civilians."

Wallstrom said that if sexual violence against women continues, it is not due to inadequacies in the laws to protect them but rather due to inadequate enforcement (*The Straits Times*, 2010).

Violation of Children's Rights: Recruitment and Use of Child Soldiers

...when armed conflict breaks out, reignites or intensifies, children will almost inevitably become involved as soldiers.

--Child Soldiers: Global Report 2008 (Coalition, 2009).

Child soldiers are a commander's dream come true: the perfect low-technology, cheap and expendable weapon system, which can perpetuate itself ad infinitum.

--Lt. Gen. Romeo Daillaire (2010).

Our discussion of violation of children's rights will deal only with the recruitment and use of child soldiers. Widespread international attention of violence towards children grew with the rise in use of child soldiers. The recruitment of child soldiers has been active in several African nations. The Capetown Principles (UNICEF, 1997) presented the following formal definition of a child soldier:

> A child soldier is any person under 18 years of age who is part of any kind of regular or irregular armed force or armed group in any capacity, including but not limited to cooks, porters, messengers and anyone accompanying such groups, other than family members. The definition includes girls recruited for sexual purposes and for forced marriage. It does not, therefore, only refer to a child who is carrying or has carried arms.

The crucial aspect of this definition is the recognition that designation as a "child soldier" is not limited to those bearing arms in battle.

The Rome Statute uses a more stringent limitation on the permitted age of soldiers listing the "conscripting or enlisting [of] children under the age of fifteen years into armed forces or groups or using them to participate actively in hostilities" as a war crime under Article 8.2.e.vii.

Table 1 shows SSA countries known to recruit and use child soldiers, male and female, and also known to subject girl soldiers to rape and other sexual violence during the period April 2004 to October 2007.

Table 1: SSA Countries Recruiting and Using Child Soldiers, April 2004-- October 2007

Male Children Actively Involved in Armed Conflict in Government Forces or Non-State Armed Groups	Girls also Involved in Combat and Non- Combat Roles	Girl Soldiers also Subjected to Rape and other Forms of Sexual Violence
Burundi		
Central African Republic	X	
Chad	X	
Cote d'Ivoire	X	X
DRC	X	X
Somalia		
Sudan		
Uganda	X	X

Source: Coalition (2009)

Of the eight countries in Table 1 using children in armed conflict, five also used girls in armed conflict while three also subjected the girls to rape and/or other forms of sexual abuse.

According to a UN Secretary General's report, refugee camps and IDP (internally displaced persons) camps have become "prime recruiting grounds" for child soldiers (UNGA, 2007). Globally, in 2008, at least 13 countries recruited internally displaced children into armed forces or armed groups (IDMC, 2009). Ban Ki-moon stated that a prime region of concern is the Chadian/Sudanese border and the refugee camps within this area. Both Chadian military groups and Sudanese militias are recruiting young children from the refugee camps in order to build their fighting capacity. These groups see children in their unprotected and neglected state as easier targets than the older persons (UNGA, 2007). It was reported that there were children fighting in the civil war (some children as young as six years old). The recruitment of child soldiers from refugee and IDP camps can be attributed to the lack of security, attention, and protection provided to those residing in refugee camps. For children who have already lost their families and their security due to the civil war, the bribe of money, food, and the sense of "family" which comes from recruiters is often too hard to deny and pass over to the next person (UNHCR, 2003). These recruiters are able to come around the refugee camps with money and the promise of food in exchange for service in the armed groups of rebels and even government backed-militias. For example, the Armee nationale tchadienne (ANT) in Chad in March 2009 offered 15 refugee children CFA 400,000 each ($900) to join them (UNSG, 2010).

According to the reports, the Sudanese militias were recruiting children from Sudanese refugee camps located across the border in Chad. Most of these children were physically tortured and forced into joining the forces. It was discovered that school teachers were among those "recruiting" children. There have been a number of steps taken towards banishing the role of child soldiers on paper; however, children are still being used in a number of armed conflicts around the world (Coalition, 2009). The UN Secretary- General, in a recent report on children and armed conflict, set out an analysis of countries with respect to their treatment of children (UNSC, 2010). The Report included a list of countries which have been listed for at least five years for armed groups operating within their borders recruiting and using child soldiers (government and rebel forces). In SSA these included: Chad, the DRC, Central African Republic, Rwanda, Somalia, Sudan and Uganda.

The UN Secretary-General's Report noted that concern has been expressed that the transitional government in Somalia and Kenyan authorities are recruiting child soldiers from the Kenyan refugee camp, Dadaab, in violation of international refugee laws (UNSG, 2010). Human Rights Watch (HRW, 2009) reported that child soldiers have been recruited openly both within, and outside of, the borders of the refugee camps. The Somali conflict has been raging since 1991, when the camps were created to receive those fleeing from the conflict. Nearly twenty years later the camps' inhabitants have swelled to over three times their capacity, and both the refugees and the authorities have grown weary of the situation. Kenyan authorities have been linked to many violations of human rights against the refugees including deportations, abuse, and child recruitment into armed forces. The Somali government has been able to manipulate the dire situation of thousands of youth living in hazardous conditions in overcrowded refugee camps to lure them into saving their nation and making money (HRW, 2010). In 2011, Kenya and Somali rebels became embroiled in heated conflict with each attacking the other on their home turf.

In July, 2010 the Darfur rebel group, the Justice and Equality Movement (JEM), "as a gesture of goodwill," signed an agreement in Geneva to stop using child soldiers. According to JEM they do not use child soldiers; however, the agreement explicitly allows UNICEF to have access to JEM camps to verify the absence of child soldiers (BBC, 2010b).

On the downbeat side, in August 2010 HRW issued a report that the Lord's Resistance Army (LRA), originally a Ugandan rebel group, has been conducting a brutal recruitment campaign in CAR and DRC over the last 18 months in which adults and children were abducted and forced into service.

VIOLATIONS OF THE RIGHTS OF DISPLACED PERSONS

Common Challenges Facing Refugees and IDPs

Some of the challenges facing displaced persons are the same whether they are refugees or internally displaced persons. Women and young girls in each group are the targets for sexual abuse and physical violence with death sometimes occurring.

For refugees, the UNHCR (2003) comments:

> Refugee women and girls are often subject to specific forms of abuse, such as rape, abduction, trafficking, or demands for sexual favors in exchange for protection, documents or assistance. Refugee children, especially girls are at even greater risk of sexual exploitation, violence and abuse.

Similar statements regarding IDPs are given by IDMC (2010): "Displaced women and children were exposed to rape and sexual violence in a number of countries…." and "Internally displaced children were particularly susceptible to risks associated with armed conflict…."

In a survey of 52 countries, IDMC (2009) found that internally displaced women and children were exposed to rape, sexual exploitation and gender- based violence in 18 of the countries. When the sexual abuse comes at the hands of armed groups, the results may result in horrific, brutal deaths. Displaced women and children may experience rape and other sexual abuse from other displaced persons, family members, local authorities, and even humanitarian workers including (although rarely) UN peacekeepers. Displaced women and children are also targets for abduction and human trafficking.

Refugee and internally displaced children, including adolescents, are targets for involuntary recruitment by armed groups and national armed forces. In IDMC's (2009) survey, IDP children were recruited into armed forces or armed groups in 13 countries.

While displacement increases the risk of sexual –based abuse for women and girls and the recruitment of children into armed forces, it is a recognized fact that these abuses are present in conflict situations for the civilian population in general, not just those who are displaced (ICRC, 2009; HRW, 2009).

In the Congo, HRW (2009) found that the total number of documented cases of civilians raped by Congolese and or the allied Rwandan army forces for January- September 2009 was 347, and the number of documented cases of civilians killed was 732. The number of documented cases of civilians raped by the rebel group, FDLR, was 290, and the number killed was 701.

When either group flees their homes, they are likely to leave their belongings behind taking only what they can carry. Their homes may be burned after they flee (or before). The loss of livelihoods for at least a period of time is a major challenge.

Both refugees and IDPs, if they are displaced long enough, will inevitably be met with tension with the "locals" as they compete for already stressed scarce resources. The resentment fuels more abuse aimed at those displaced persons. This heightens the importance of another challenge for both groups of DPs in determining solutions to their displacement. UNHCR (2009) estimates that there are about 5.7 million protracted refugee situations across at least 22 countries where a protracted refugee situation is defined "as one in which 25,000 or more refugees of the same nationality have been in exile for five years or more in a given asylum country." (UNHCR, 2009)

IDMC (2009) states that the majority of global IDPs live in protracted displacement and are located in some 35 different countries where protracted internal displacement situations "are those in which the processes of finding durable solutions have stalled and/or IDPs are marginalized as a consequence of violations or lack of protection of human rights, including economic, social and cultural rights." (IDMC, 2009) Unlike protracted refugee situations, protracted IDP situations do not require a minimum number of people or a minimum time.

Challenges Facing IDPs

There is no single international agency to champion the cause of the IDPs. Nor is there an international convention stipulating the rights of IDPs. The situation improved somewhat with the production of the 1998 Guiding Principles on Internal Displacement, the 2004 creation of the position of Representative of the Secretary General on the Human rights of Internally Displaced Persons and the adoption of the Cluster Approach in 2005 whereby the UNHCR assumes some responsibility for IDPs. However, only a fraction of IDPs actually receive assistance from the UNHCR as shown in Table 2. IDMC (2009) found that in at least 26 countries IDPs still faced violence in their area of refuge. The rationale for the lack of a single body is the principle of sovereignty in which domestic governments are expected to protect their own civilians and IDPs. However, as discussed above, the government and its armed forces may be the perpetrators of the abuse including killings of members of both groups.

Statistical information on IDPs is inadequate. For example, the 11.6 million IDP figure for Africa is based on information from just 19 countries. Eight countries denied the existence of IDPs caused by conflict, generalized violence or human rights violations, and 36 countries denied the forced displacement of ethnic minorities (IDMC, 2009). Up to date information for 2008 was available in only six countries. "For the rest, data was outdated, incomplete or non-existent" (IDMC, 2009). Urban IDPs are difficult to distinguish from other migrants and the urban poor. Many IDPs do not register their status in order to preserve their anonymity; however in failing to register, they also forego whatever assistance may be available for them.

Challenges Facing Refugees

Women and children account for 80% of the refugee population. Refugee women tend to have cultural and educational handicaps. They generally are illiterate and have little or no prior work experience. These handicaps make it more difficult for the women to complete necessary forms for refugee status. Women suffer ongoing trauma from just being a refugee. Women and children receive unequal (i.e. inequitable) allocations of provisions in the camps (Harris, 2000).

While refugees have the advantages of having a formal body, the Office of the UNHCR, charged with protecting refugees and an established international convention (the 1951 Convention), which stipulates the rights of refugees, unfortunately, the rights set forth in the 1951 Convention are frequently breached.

Refugee Rights Report Card

The USCRI (2009) produced a "Refugee Rights Report Card" which scored 52 countries on the elements of refugee protection (in the 1951 Convention) within their countries. The four classifications for which the countries were graded, along with the associated grading systems, follow:

I. Refoulement/Physical Protection,
   - A: No *refoulement*; fair asylum system
   - B: No *refoulement* but faulty asylum systems
   - C: Some *refoulement* but not systematic; governmental harassment and serious physical risk;
   - D: Systematic *refoulement*; governmental violence against refugees
   - F: 100+ *refoulements*; severe governmental violence

II. Detention/Access to Courts,
   - A: No arbitrary detention; access to courts and documentation
   - B: Little detention
   - C: Significant detention; faulty access to courts and documentation
   - D: More than 100 arbitrarily detained
   - F: More than 200 arbitrarily detained; no access to courts

III. Freedom of Movement and Residence,
   - A: No restrictions in policy or practice
   - B: Almost no restrictions in policy or practice
   - C: Restrictions in policy but wide tolerance
   - D: Restrictions in policy and practice; harassment
   - F: Severe restrictions in policy and practice

IV. Right to earn a Livelihood,
   - A: No restrictions in policy or practice
   - B: Almost no restrictions in Policy or practice
   - C: Restrictions in policy but wide tolerance in practice
   - D: Restrictions in policy and practice; harassment
   - F: Severe restrictions in Policy and practice

Space does not permit a treatment of all four Tables scoring the countries provided by USCRI (2009). Table 2 provides the list of those countries which scored only A's or B's on each classification as representing best performers. Similarly, those scoring only D's and F's on are deemed the poorest performers (author's choice of categories).

Table 2: Best and Worst performers, and Europe and US Performance on Refugee Protection

Country	Refoulement/ Physical Protection	Detention/ Access to Courts	Freedom of Movement and Residence	Right to Earn a Livelihood
BEST PERFORMERS				
Brazil	A	A	A	A
Niger	A	A	A	B
Costa Rica	A	B	A	A
Canada	B	B	A	A
POOREST PERFORMERS				
Iran	F	D	F	F
Malaysia	F	F	D	F
Thailand	F	F	F	D
Kenya	F	D	F	D
Turkey	F	F	D	D
EUROPE & US				
Europe	D	D	B	B
United States	F	D	A	A

Source: USCRI (2009)

Surprisingly, and disappointingly, the set of Best Performing countries contained only four countries: Brazil (4 A's), Niger (3 A's and 1 B), Costa Rica (3 A's and 1 B) and Canada, (2 A's and 2 B's). Similarly, the poorest performers include: Iran (4 F's), Malaysia (1 D, and 3 F's), Thailand (1 D, and 3 F's), Kenya (2 D's and 2 F's) and Turkey (2 D's and 2 F's).

Table 2 also includes the US and Europe neither of which falls into the Best or Worst performer categories, but they are included in Table 2 for interest. Both countries fail on I and II. Europe scores a D rating on both of these items, while the US scores an F on I and a D on II.

The USCRI result is a set of four refugee Rights Report Cards, one for each "Rights" component, and with each containing 52 countries associated with their respective score. The USCRI Report Card for the Refoulement/Physical Protection category is given below for illustrative purposes.

Table 3: Refoulement/Physical Protection

GRADES	A	B	C	D	F
COUNTRIES BY GRADE	Botswana	Burundi	Algeria	Chad	China
	Brazil	Canada	Bangladesh	Europe	Congo, D.R.
	Costa Rica	Rep. of Congo	Cameroon	Iraq	Egypt
	Malawi	Cote d'Ivoire	Ghana	Israel	Israeli-occupied territories
	Niger	Ecuador	India	Pakistan	Iran
		Ethiopia	Jordan	Panama	Kenya
		Guinea	Mauritania	Russia	Lebanon
		Kuwait	Nepal	Saudi Arabia	Libya
		Senegal	Rwanda	Sudan	Malaysia
		Serbia	Venezuela	Syria	South Africa
		Tanzania	Zambia		Thailand
		Uganda			Turkey
					United States
					Yemen

Source: USCRI (2009)

While the four Tables contain valuable information for assessing the accountability of host countries, the information, as presented, is not very convenient for subsequent analysis. Analysts or other interested readers need to go through each of the four tables picking out their country or countries of interest along with the set of respective scores. In order to make this more convenient, a single Report Card for the set of host countries along with their respective scores can be generated using the information contained in the four Tables. The resulting matrix would have dimensions: 53X5 including country names and category labels. Given space constraints, and the size of the full table, a stylized version with selected countries arranged alphabetically is given in Table 4. The readers may complete the rest of the table. As can be seen, despite its size, this table makes it very easy to examine individual countries since all scores appear with the respective country (for the full table, see Forster, 2011a).

A Grade Point Average (GPA) Approach

Notice that Brazil scores an A for every component. It is the only country with a straight- A performance. Most countries have scores that vary across the four components. Faced with different scores across the components, how does one assess "overall performance" of the host country? Forster (2011a, b) proposed the use a "country equivalent" to a student's Grade Point Average (GPA) which is well-known to US schools. For those not familiar with GPAs as summary measures of student performance, some brief comments may help. First, each letter grade is associated with a numerical score A=4; B=3; C=2; D=1; and F=0. Having assigned each component score with a number score, calculate the average score across the set of scores for each country. This GPA is a measure of the average performance of the country, and hence, is a measure of overall performance of the respective country. Country-specific GPAs are given in the far right-hand column of Table 4.

We now have 52 individual indicators of overall performance. The next question is how to assess the overall compliance of the entire group of host countries. The information in Table 4 could be rearranged easily to produce a Table in which countries are listed not alphabetically but rather in descending order by GPAs (another exercise for the reader to complete, or see Forster (2011a)). The analyst can then select an appropriate cut-off GPA, say 3.0, or maybe 2.5 – analyst's choice. Now, determine how many countries score above/below the cut-off? Alternatively, what is the *proportion* of countries scoring above/below the cut-off? These numbers can serve as indicators of overall performance of the group.

Table 4: Measures of Host Country Compliance with Refugee Rights

Country (in alphabetical order)	Refoulement/ Physical Protection	Detention/ Access to Courts	Freedom of Movement and Residence	Right to Earn a Livelihood	GPA
1. Algeria	C	D	F	F	**0.75**
2. Bangladesh	C	D	D	C	**1.5**
3. Brazil	A	A	A	A	**4.0**

------					
25. Jordan	C	D	A	D	**2.0**
26. Kenya	F	D	F	D	**0.5**
27. Kuwait	B	A	B	D	**2.75**

------					
50. Venezuela	C	C	C	B	**2.25**
51. Yemen	F	D	C	C	**1.25**
52. Zambia	C	B	D	D	**1.75**

Source: Author's Creation Based upon USCRI (2009)

An alternative approach is to compute the average GPA for the group and this becomes the overall performance measure. However, we can invoke a piece of information that will affect (and simplify) how we grade countries performance for the present case. In a 2007 Introductory Note to the 1951 Convention, the Office of the UNHCR states that the principle of *non-refoulement* is considered to be sufficiently fundamental that **no deviation is acceptable** (emphasis added). If this condition is invoked in the grade assessment process then any country that scores a C, D or F on the question of refoulement receives a failing grade overall. This means that we can start with the *non-refoulement* component, and consider only those countries scoring an A or a B. As can be seen from Table 1, only 17 of the 52 countries survive this first test. This means that only one-third of the group performs satisfactorily. The rest of the countries, having deviated from the non-refoulement requirement, receive a failing grade, or a 0 overall. This is similar to a student failing a required course in the program of study and who fails out of the program as a result. Now compute the average grade using the GPAs for the 17 satisfactory countries and a score of 0 for remaining 35. The average grade for the 17 acceptable countries is 2.77 which meets the 2.50 criterion but not the 3.0 one. The average grade for all 52 countries falls to 0.9 which is below a D-level performance for the group overall.

The results presented here could not be gleaned by just looking at the four Tables in USCRI's report. Those Tables provide the raw data. The GPA provides a vehicle for extracting additional penetrating insight to the Refugee Rights Compliance of individual countries and of the set of host countries together.

USCRI (2009) also presents a section entitled "Best and Worst Places for Refugees." This section provides no scoring per se for the reader providing instead a set of narratives. The following countries would be considered in the Best category: Brazil, Ecuador, and Costa Rica. Those in the Worst category included: Gaza, Thailand, Kenya, Malaysia, Egypt, and Turkey.

Country Narratives

The following direct quotes from USCRI (2009) provide country-specific examples of the breaching of the 1951 Convention:

Thailand.

> When Thailand's navy intercepted boats carrying a reported 992 Myanmarese Rohingya in December, they detained the already weak and hungry refugees and reportedly kicked and beat them. They then forced them back onto their unseaworthy boats, towed them out to sea, and abandoned them without engines and scant food or water…..It also continued to deport thousands of Myanmarese back to their home country.

Kenya.

> Since 2007, Kenya has attempted to keep its border with Somalia closed to refugees fleeing violence there with little success. ….They also beat Somalis and demanded bribes from them when they caught them trying to reach the camp complex at Dadaab.

Malaysia.

> Malaysian immigration officials continued to sell deportees to gangs that operate along the Malaysia-Thailand border. …..At least 1,000 refugees and asylum seekers were among the deportees in 2008.

Egypt.

> Egyptian border guards shot and killed as many as 33 African migrants trying to cross the Sinai Peninsula into Israel....Egypt also forcibly returned as many as 1,400 Eritreans and returned Sudanese who had been to Israel despite Sudan's penalties for travel to Israel including long-term imprisonment or death.

THE SUM OF ALL FEARS: PHYSICAL, EMOTIONAL AND PSYCHOLOGICAL DAMAGE

The worst scars are in the mind

> --Reyes (2007)

Post-Traumatic Stress Disorder (PTSD)

PTSD has been with us for a long time under different names

> --General Michael Chiarrelli, Vice Chief of Staff, U.S. Army, on CNN's State of the Union, May 29, 2011.

Most adults in the English speaking world are likely familiar with the PTSD acronym, and have a general idea of its meaning while (perhaps) not fully understanding all of the medical implications that have been uncovered since its recognition. As General Chiarrelli comments, the phenomenon has been around for a long time but with various names. In terms of relatively recent history, the phenomenon was noted in the US Civil War, and was called Soldiers' Heart.

In WWI the phenomenon was known as Shell Shock, Combat Fatigue or Battle Fatigue. Symptoms could lead troops to flee a battle site, and then they may face accusations of cowardice or desertion. In WWI, treatment these symptoms could be swift and brutal. Three hundred and six British and Commonwealth soldiers were executed by firing squad for exhibiting the signs of Shell Shock. Only recently (in 2006!) have those soldiers received pardons for their behavior. Some soldiers executed were as young as 16 years of age. Gross Stress Syndrome was the term used in WWII.

In the 1970s, the medical community began to notice behavioral issues with American soldiers returning from the war in Vietnam. The phenomenon was termed Post-Vietnam Syndrome. It would take until 1980 for the phenomenon to be recognized formally by the American Psychiatry Association as a legitimate medical diagnosis, and PTSD blazed onto the scene and into our collective minds.

A relatively simple definition of PTSD is "an emotional illness that is classified as an anxiety disorder and usually develops as a result of a terribly frightening, life-threatening, or otherwise highly unsafe experience."

As the foregoing discussion highlights, PTSD and its precursors were viewed as problems confronting combatants. Since recognizing PTSD as a medical diagnosis in 1980, the medical profession has come to realize that PTSD is not a condition reserved solely for combatants. It is believed that 7%-8% of people in the US will suffer from PTSD in their lives, with women experiencing rates double those of males. For combatants and rape victims the rates vary between 10% and 30%. Up to 100% of children who witnessed the killing of a parent or endured a sexual assault or abuse may develop PTSD (MN, undated).

HR (2007) noted that:

> Being displaced can have severe adverse effects on the physical, social, emotional and spiritual well-being of a person. Exposure to violence or disaster, loss of or separation from family members and friends, deterioration in living conditions, the inability to provide for one's self and family, and the lack of access to services, can all have immediate and long-term consequences for individuals, families, and communities, including post-traumatic stress disorders, psychosomatic illness, depression, anxiety, and even violence.

Other studies have shown that the impact of sexual violence on children is associated with "lower social competence," "lower academic performance" and "lower self-esteem" (IASC, 2007).

TWO HIGH-PROFILE COUNTRIES

Darfur, Sudan

Approximately 2.5 million people from Darfur were displaced due to the civil conflict; several have become refugees in Cairo, Egypt. The Meffert and Marmar (2008) study concerning the mental health of the refugees found that a large number of Darfur refugees had "undergone intense traumatic exposure, including rape, murder of family members, and narrow escape from death." Short term impacts of the experiences of the refugees lead to many depression- related symptoms such as "hopelessness, tearfulness, apathy, decreased concentration, decreased or increased sleep, low appetite, weight loss, low mood, decreased energy, and guilt." The refugees were found to have a higher rate of PTSD and other disorders than general population due to their experiences. These "experiences may have significant negative effects on their sense of worth and general self-esteem." The study found a higher level of conflict within families (both husbands with wives and parents with children) as well as higher levels of violence amongst youth.

Without a strong support system, the result is "a lack of independence, unemployment, legal involvement, family dysfunction and disintegration, and a minimal social support system." The traumatic events that many displaced people experience prior to, or as part of their displacement, lead to many physical and mental impacts that may have lasting impact on their future livelihood and contribution to their new home once resettled.

Democratic Republic of Congo

The Democratic Republic of Congo has earned the reputation of being the rape capital of the world. Rape is a strategic weapon of war, which is very apparent in the Congo. Many years after the civil war ended in the Congo in 2003, the trend of using rape to control, intimidate and displace citizens has not improved. For example, during the military operations against FDLR militia between Jan and October 2009, more than 1,000 civilians were killed, 7,000 women and girls were raped, more than 6,000 homes were destroyed and nearly 900,000 have been displaced and forced to live in squalid displacement camps (HRW, 2009). In a particularly cold-blooded and systematic attack in August 2010, 300 people were raped, 235 of the people were women, 52 were girls, 13 were men and 3 were boys. In the raid, 116 people were abducted.
Peterman et al. (2011) found that approximately 1.7-1.8 million women were raped in their lifetime. This report illustrated that rape is becoming more prevalent among civilians than previously thought as well as projecting that about 3.1-3.4 million women report sexual violence with their intimate partner. It has been found that over 400,000 people report being raped in the preceding year, while previous UN estimate was 16,000 in one year.

As if the brutality endured within the Congo is not enough, migrant Congolese women along the Angola-Congo border are suffering "vicious measures" undertaken by Angolans designed to get rid of the Congolese. Between April and August 2011, Angolan women experienced some

"21,000 cases of serious human rights violations including rape, beating and torture and looting" (*The Economist*, 2011).

GENERAL ASSESSMENT OF DAMAGES

As noted above, Collier states that "civil war is economic development in reverse." The major reason for this assessment is the impact that civil war has on the economy's factors of production: human resources, physical capital and natural resources.

The most obvious negative impacts on human resources occur as combat and collateral deaths. These losses are forever! The term "brain drain" refers to the loss of a country's human capital to other countries. The human capital in this case refers to the skills and educational training embodied in those leaving the country. In the typical story the individuals exit less developed countries and migrate voluntarily to more developed countries to take advantage of higher compensation levels. In times of war these individuals may still leave voluntarily, but the prime reason may be to relocate in safer environments (even if financial compensation is comparable to those at home). These individuals are usually highly talented and have the financial ability to move voluntarily. This voluntary migration reduces the productive labor force in the less developed countries and reduces their economic growth potential. However, in the brain drain case the amount of human capital is unchanged globally. There is just a redistribution of the global supply of human capital. Host countries benefit from the expansion of their labor pool.

Those who are involuntarily displaced, as refugees or IDPs, face other difficulties since they are at elevated risk of further safety problems discussed above. The psychological and emotional damages have long-lasting debilitating consequences that reduce their productive capabilities

The parties to the civil conflict compete for control of the country's natural resources either to fund their military exploits or to line their own pockets. Either way, the resources are diverted away from socially productive use. The nature of warfare destroys physical assets including structures (housing and production facilities) which also reduce the productive capacity of affected countries.

REFERENCES

BBC NEWS (BBC) 2009a. African Union in rift with court. 7-3-2009. newsvote.bbc.co.uk. Retrieved 7-3-2009.

BBC NEWS (BBC) 2009b. Arab leaders back 'wanted' Bashir. 3-30-2009. newsvote.bbc.co.uk. Retrieved 3-31-2009.

BBC NEWS (BBC). 2010a. ICC refers Sudan war crimes cases to UN. 5-26-2010. www.newsbbc.co.uk. Retrieved 5-26-2010.

BBC NEWS (BBC). Africa 2010b. Darfur JEM rebels sign deal to stop child soldiers. 7-21-2010. www.bbc.co.uk/news/world-africa. Retrieved 7-21-2010.

Burgess, A. 2004. Health Challenges for Refugees and Immigrants. IRSA, Research Reports, March/April.

Cheadle, D. and Prendergast, J. 2007. *Not On Our Watch: The Mission to End Genocide In Darfur And Beyond.* The Write Element and John Prendergast.

Coalition to Stop the Use of Child Soldiers (Coalition) 2009. *Child soldiers: global report 2008.* www.childsoldiersglobalreport.org/overview-and-benchmarks. Retrieved 11-19-2009.

Collier, P. 2007. *The Bottom Billion.* Oxford University Press. New York, NY.

Daillaire, R. 2010. *They Fight Like Soldiers. They Die like Children.* Random House Canada.

Daillaire, R. with Beardsley, B. 2004. *Shake Hands with the Devil.* Vintage Canada

The Economist. 2011. Angola and Congo: Bad Neighbours. August 6, 2011. 39

Forster, B.A. 2011a. Report Cards on Refugees' Rights. *Forced Migration Review.* 37 Online. www.fmreview.org . (This version contains two large Tables not included in the print version)

Forster, B.A. 2011b. Report Cards on Refugees' Rights. *Forced Migration Review.* 37, 57-58.

Gambino, A. W. 2008. *Congo: Securing Peace, Sustaining Progress.* Council on Foreign Relations. Special Report No. 40

Harris, J. P. 2000. Refugee Women: Failing to Find Solutions. *Human Rights Brief,* 7(3)www.wcl.american.edu/hrbrief/v7i3/rape.htm

Harvard Humanitarian Initiative (HHI) 2010. "Now, the world is without me": an investigation of sexual violence in eastern democratic republic of Congo. Harvard Humanitarian Initiative, and Oxfam.

Humanitarian Reform (HR). 2007. www.humanitarianreform.org

Human Rights Watch (HRW). 2009. DR Congo: Civilian Cost of Military Operation is Unacceptable. www.hrw.org/en/news/2009/10/12/dr-congo-civilian-cost-miltary-operation-unaccept.

The Inter-Agency Standing Committee (IASC). (2007). *IASC Guidelines on Mental Health and Psychosocial Support in Emergency Settings 2007.* Geneva, IASC.

Internal Displacement Monitoring Center (IDMC). 2009. Internal Displacement: Global Overview of Trends and Development in 2008.

Internal Displacement Monitoring Center (IDMC). 2010. Internal Displacement: Global Overview of Trends and Development in 2009.

Internal Displacement Monitoring Center (IDMC). 2011. Internal Displacement: Global Overview of Trends and Development in 2010.

MedicineNet(MN). undated. www.medicinenet.com/posttraumatic_stress_disorder/article.htm

Meffert, S.M. & Marmar, C. R. 2009. Darfur Refugees in Cairo: Mental Health and Interpersonal Conflict in the Aftermath of Genocide. *Journal of Interpersonal Violence*, 24(11), 1835-1848.

Office of the Special Adviser on the Prevention of Genocide (OSAPG), 2009. Prevention of genocide. Booklet on what is genocide, why it happens and what is the role of the Special Adviser of the Secretary General, the United Nations system and the International Criminal Court. UN Department of Public Information / the Office of the Special Adviser on the Prevention of Genocide. February 2009. www.un.org/preventgenocide/adviser .

Schlein, L. 2010. Rape in DRC Reaches Alarming Levels. *Voice of America*, www.voanews.com

Strumpen-Darrie, C. 2000. Rape: A Survey of Current International Jurisprudence. 7 (3)www.wcl.american.edu/hrbrief/v7i3/rape.htm

United Nations High Commissioner for Human Rights (UNHCHR). 1998. Guiding Principles on Internal Displacement. www.unhchr.ch Retrieved 3-21-2009.

United Nations High Commissioner for Refugees (UNHCR). 2002. UNHCR Releases 2001 Global Refugee Statistics. Press Releases. June 18, 2002.

United Nations High Commissioner for Refugees (UNHCR). 2003. Agenda for Protection.

United Nations High Commissioner for Refugees (UNHCR). 2004. UNHCR: Sharp Decline In Refugees, Others Of Concern In 2003. Press Releases. June 17, 2004.

United Nations High Commissioner for Refugees (UNHCR). 2005. 2004 Global Refugee Trends.

United Nations High Commissioner for Refugees (UNHCR). 2006. 2005 Global Refugee Trends.

United Nations High Commissioner for Refugees (UNHCR). 2007b. 2006 Global Trends: Refugees, Asylum Seekers, Returnees, Internally Displaced and Stateless Persons.

United Nations High Commissioner for Refugees (UNHCR). 2008. 2007 Global Trends:Refugees, Asylum Seekers, Returnees, Internally Displaced and Stateless Persons.

United Nations High Commissioner for Refugees (UNHCR). 2009. 2008 Global Trends:Refugees, Asylum Seekers, Returnees, Internally Displaced and Stateless Persons.

United Nations High Commissioner for Refugees (UNHCR). 2010. 2009 Global Trends:Refugees, Asylum Seekers, Returnees, Internally Displaced and Stateless Persons.

UNICEF 1997. The Capetown principles and best practices on the prevention of recruitment of children into the armed forces and on the demobilization and reintegration of child soldiers in Africa. April 1997.

United Nations Relief and Works Agency for Palestine Refugees in the Near East (UNRWA). 2009. UNRWA Fact sheet. www.unrwa.org.

United Nations Security Council Report (UNSC). 2006. Protection of Civilians in Armed Conflict. Update Report 5, June 21.

United Nations Security Council Report (UNSC). 2007. Children and Armed Conflict. www.un.org December 21.

United Nations Security Council Report (UNSC), 2007. Children and Armed Conflict. www.un.org April 13.

United Nations General Assembly (UNGA) 1948. Convention on the Prevention and Punishment of The Crime Of Genocide. www.unhchr.ch Retrieved 5-17-2009.

United Nations Secretary-General (UNSG), 2009. Implementing the Responsibility to Protect: Report of the Secretary-General. UN General Assembly.

United Nations Secretary-General (UNSG) 2010. Children and Armed Conflict: Report of the Secretary-General. UN General Assembly.

United Nations (UN) 2002. Rome Statute of The International Criminal Court.

United Nations High Commissioner for Refugees (UNHCR). 2010. UNHCR Condemns Endemic Rape In DRC, Helps Survivors. www.unhcr.org/print/4bd18e7e9.html . Retrieved 7-29-2010

CHAPTER 9
PLAUSIBLE EXPLANATIONS FOR THE FAILURE TO RESPECT, OR TO ENFORCE, INTERNATIONAL LAWS

SELF-INTEREST

Games People Play

Economists studying public policy formation have long been cognizant of the influence that the self-interests of the participating agents has on the process. Using an extension of Hartle's (1983) concept of "intersecting games" in government decision-making to the civil conflict situation provides a framework for thinking about predatory behavior and natural resources. Hartle's approach identifies the relevant groups having special interests in the outcome. Each group seeks to maximize their own utility playing by the rules of their own game. For example, we can consider a given country's own population as being partitioned into three groups: a group aligned with the government, a group aligned with some rebel organization and a group of non-aligned people. The first two groups can also be partitioned into the elite ruling members of the group, the armed forces and the civilian population sympathetic to the respective elite group. The non-aligned are the civilians who do not have allegiance to either the government or the rebel group. In any event they can become targets or instruments for either side. The government group wants to retain ruling control while the rebels seek to overthrow the government and become the new government. These groups will settle on their rules of the game to retain or gain the right to govern and reap the associated benefits. Outright lying may become part of their strategy. The excuse for conflict can be given as an attempt to achieve justice for example rather than showing greed. They may blame ethnic bias or religious intolerance. The big reward is the power and control of valuable assets. They will exploit the non-aligned to bolster their fighting base. They will use terror to control civilians. They can be expected to deny the nasty while trying to sound altruistic.

Sieff (2008) is quite blunt in her assessment of the motives and behavior of the Nigerian rebel group Mend (Movement for the Emancipation of the Niger Delta) stating:

> *For years, the group has claimed it desires "total control" of Nigeria's oil wealth in order to end poverty and misery in the*

> *Delta. But MEND is not the Robin Hood it makes itself out to be. Its main activity is the kidnapping of foreign oil workers, held for ransoms; and, to my knowledge, these revenues are not distributed to the men, women, and children who live in horrific poverty across the region.*

Sieff also notes that some in the media are co-opted into being "cause believers":

> *...the well-intentioned writers and activists who dare to report on these dangerous conflicts in faraway lands are usually of a liberal persuasion, and continue to see "freedom fighters" when, in truth, most are common thugs.*

Rawlsian Justice

The African support for Bashir has a "Rawlsian" feel about it. In the Rawls (1971) theory of justice, agents consider themselves behind a veil of ignorance, and they must design a mechanism for the allocation of resources. The Rawls contention is that with everyone placed behind a veil of ignorance, and hence not knowing which allocation in Society they would receive, the optimum allocation mechanism for each individual is one that ensured the least advantaged position was made as well-off as any other position. Using this thought process for Africa, one can see that all leaders could fear that what was happening to Bashir might just as easily happen to themselves. So they want him to be as well off as possible to protect themselves at some later time. When, in 2011, Qaddafi was being pressured to step down by the combined countries of NATO and some Arab countries, the Sudan expressed its support for Libya and Qaddafi. This looks like a quid pro quo for Libya having supported Bashir against the ICC earlier.

Another approach is to think of Africa, or the African Union, as a club. It is not surprising that, when faced with outside interference, the members of the club close ranks against the outsiders.

It is very interesting to note that the bonds were breaking for some members in 2010 and 2011. In particular, AU troops intervened in Somalia, and called for outside assistance. Kenya took on the rebels from Somalia. The club split over Libya. The AU suspended Cote d'Ivoire (Ivory Coast) due to the dispute over the election and Gbagbo's refusal to step down after losing the election (BBC NEWS, 2010a).

NATURAL RESOURCES AND PREDATORY BEHAVIOR

Collier (2007) noted that the "Dependence upon primary commodity exports—oil, diamonds, and the like –substantially increases the risk of civil war." Collier suggests that valuable natural resources leads to predatory behavior defined as the "use of force to extort goods or money from their legitimate owners." Predation may enhance the lifestyles of the predators and/or finance their side of a conflict (Collier, 2000). The "owners" have an incentive to retain control of the natural resource assets, and rebel forces have an incentive to gain control of the assets. Economists also describe predatory behavior as rent-seeking behavior. Control of these assets becomes a source of conflict between rival groups. Table 2 lists SAA countries possessing selected types of valuable natural resources. Some SSA countries have deposits of highly valued resource assets.

Table 1: Selected Natural Resources Possessed by SAA Countries

NATURAL RESOURCE	SSA COUNTRIES
Diamonds	Angola, Botswana, Congo, Cote d'Ivoire, DR Congo, Liberia, Namibia, Sierra Leone, South Africa, Tanzania
Gold	Burundi, Congo, DR Congo, Eritrea Ethiopia, Ghana, Mali, Namibia, Rwanda, South Africa
Iron Ore	Guinea, Liberia, Niger, Nigeria, Senegal, Sierra Leone, Sudan, Tanzania, Tunisia, Western Sahara
Petroleum	Angola, Benin, Cameroon, Congo, Cote d'Ivoire, Equatorial Guinea, Gabon, Nigeria, Sudan
Uranium	Chad, Namibia, Somalia, South Africa

Source: Developed from *Exploring Africa*

The UPC, led by Thomas Lubanga, under ICC indictment for the use of child soldiers, was one of six groups fighting for control of the gold-rich Ituri region (BBC, 2010b). A Rwandan rebel group, the Democratic Forces for the Liberation of Rwanda (FDLR), is operating in the eastern Congo and is believed to be making millions by controlling gold and other mineral mines, and by using extortion to take money from the local population (BBC, 2010b). Fessy (2010) reported that a senior DR Congo officer, General Amisi Kumba, installed a mining firm, Geminaco, at a gold mine in eastern DR Congo. In return for this assistance General Kumba would receive a 25% share of the monthly production of raw gold. Echoing the message of this section of the paper Fessy wrote "The lure of profits from mines in Eastern DR Congo has turned the area into a battlefield."

Foreign Interests

There also may be foreign players involved in the game who support one or other side in order to protect their own access to the assets. They also play by their own rules to maximize their well-being. The foreign players include individual countries and world bodies such as the IMF, the WTO and a host of NGOs such as humanitarian agencies. China has been investing heavily in developing countries around the world "building a string of alliances across the globe with countries overlooked and sometimes shunned by the United States..." (Halper, 2010). Halper (2010) further states, "While the USA and European gurus are busy lecturing Third World autocrats about good governance and transparency, Chinese engineers are building highways to the dictators' weekend homes." China is quietly buying votes from its new allies to have them back the Chinese positions in key world bodies. Countries which do not fall in line with China's position risk losing their Chinese funding. China's largest regional commitment is Africa. China has been a major ally of the Sudanese government in the case of Darfur, and it has opposed the ICC decision to indict President al-Bashir.

India seems to have taken a page from the Chinese "Handbook." India is expected to diversify its oil sources to include Africa. Other resources of interest to India from African countries include diamonds, gold, coal and uranium. India is the third-largest contributor of peacekeeping forces to Africa (in Sudan and Congo), and the Indian navy is involved in patrolling for Somali pirates (as is China's). India is also providing loans to Africa including some funding to pay for education and railways. This is ironic since India is a recipient of foreign aid itself and much in need of improvements in social infrastructure. India expects support from Africa in becoming a permanent member of the UN Security Council (*The Economist*, 2011a).

The US has softened its position on Sudan since having cited it for practicing genocide. Sudan, a former base for Osama bin Laden, is offering to help the US in the war on terror. It has been suggested that the US has traded off its humanitarian support for Darfur in return for Sudan's assistance with terror issues.

Industrial Interests

Another group that has a vested interest in various assets is the set of firms involved in the extraction of these assets, and in the marketing of such products. One such example is the diamond market where the diamond industry, the UN, and NGOs (non-government organizations), and respective governments of diamond producing countries created a mechanism in 2003, known as the Kimberly Process (KP), for halting the flow of conflict diamonds to the world market. Oppenheimer (2008) suggests that KP has been successful with 99% of world diamond production being conflict free. Not everyone is a fan, however. Rotberg's (2010) assessment is that "The toothless Kimberley Process, an international initiative meant to segregate blood diamonds from non-conflict diamonds, has failed to stop stolen Zimbabwean diamonds from entering the world market." Perhaps this is the other 1%? Notice the choice of language. Rotberg uses the emotive "blood" diamonds while Oppenheimer uses "conflict diamonds" which is much softer in tone. Oppenheimer declared a special interest. He is chairman of the De Beers mining company–the world's largest diamond producer. De Beers got started in South Africa 120 years ago on the Kimberley diamond fields (Oppenheimer, 2008).

In the summer of 2011, the Kimberley Process came under a dark cloud, and it is in danger of collapse (*The Economist*, 2011b). The controversy is due to a unilateral decision by the KP's chairman to allow two Zimbabwean-South African joint ventures to resume diamond sales.
Such decisions are normally made by consensus. Opponents of the decision point to human-rights abuses and other breaches of the KP's rules. The NGO Global Witness withdrew from the KP in December 2011 "saying the Kimberly Process has failed to break the link between diamond sales and violence" (BBC, 2011). Poor countries view the KP as a Western plot to control trade in diamonds to their detriment (*The Economist*, 2011b).

STATE SOVEREIGNTY

The concept of sovereignty as we know it in modern times traces its heritage to the signing of the Treaties of Westphalia in 1648 which ended the Thirty Years War in Europe. Sovereignty refers to the (expected) competence, independence, and legal equality of states (IDRC, undated). Derivative of the concept of sovereignty is the principle of noninterference in the internal affairs of other sovereign states (IDRC, undated).

The sovereignty concept is endorsed by the Charter of the United Nations Article 2(1): "The Organization is based on the principle of sovereign equality of all its members." The Shanghai Cooperation Organization (SCO), comprised of China, Russia, Kazakhstan, Kyrgystan, Tajikistan, and Uzbekistan, also adopted sovereignty as one of its principles. The set of principles includes "respect for each other's independence, sovereignty and territorial integrity, non-interference in each other's internal affairs, mutual non-use or threat of use of force; equality among all member states…."(MFAPRC, 2004). Scraping away the fancy language involving mutual respect and territorial integrity, we can sum up as follows: "If you leave us alone to do whatever we want to do, we'll leave you alone too."

Above we noted that China has been busy building a coalition of countries which will vote as China desires in key world forums. Halper (2010) notes that one such area of concern is for China's position on human rights issues, and "Many of these same countries have joined to vigorously defend traditional sovereignty-- a notion deeply important to Beijing because it fears, and resents, what it sees as Western meddling in its internal affairs. Support for China and Russia on this issue [human rights] has exceeded 80% in recent years." This is an example of how the concept of sovereignty can be used to block interference. It matters not whether the nations really value sovereignty, it suffices as a tool to justify being left alone to do what they wish and argue that international standards need not apply to them.

Sovereignty also offers western nations a convenient reason to not interfere in the affairs of other sovereign states to assist the oppressed. Other countries use State sovereignty to justify inaction. Chad, an ICC member country, announced in July 2010 that it would not arrest Bashir during a visit to Chad. Chad's Minister of the Interior and Security justified its inaction by explaining that "Chad is a sovereign and independent state…" This move would make Chad the first ICC country to harbor a suspected criminal from the Court (BBC, 2010c). Kenya joined Chad in the summer of 2010 when it refused to arrest Bashir while he was in Kenya when the country adopted a new constitution (BBC, 2010d). Chad and Kenya seem to have "conveniently" forgotten their obligations under the terms of Article 1of the Genocide Convention as elaborated by the OSAPG (2009) discussed above.

REFERENCES

BBC NEWS (BBC): Africa. 2010a. African Union suspends Ivory Coast over disputed poll. 12-9-2010. www.bbc.co.uk/news/world-africa . Retrieved 12-9-2010.

BBC NEWS (BBC): Africa. 2010b. Thomas Lubanga: ICC Trial of DR Congo warlord to resume. 10-8 -2010. www.bbc.co.uk/news/world-africa . Retrieved 10-8-2010.

BBC NEWS (BBC). 2010c. 'No question' of Chad arresting Sudan President Bashir. 7-22-2010. www.bbc.co.uk/news/world-africa .

BBC NEWS (BBC). 2010d. Court worry at Omar al-Bashir's Kenya trip. 8-27-2010.www.bbc.co.uk/news/world-africa

BBC NEWS (BBC). 2011. Global Witness leaves Kimberly Process diamond scheme. 12-5-2011.www.bbc.co.uk/news/business

Collier, P. 2000. Economic causes of civil conflict and their implications for policy. Manuscript, World Bank.

Collier, P. 2007. *The Bottom Billion.* Oxford University Press, New York.

The Economist. 2011a. India in Africa: Catching up. 5-28-2011. 47-48.

The Economist. 2011b. Zimbabwe and its Diamonds: Forever Dirty. 7-2-2011. p. 40.

Exploring Africa. Undated. Agricultural and Mineral Resources Table. http//Exploringafrica.matrix.msu.edu

Fessy, T. 2010. Congo General Profits from Blood Gold. BBC NEWS AFRICA. www.bbc.co.uk 11-10-2010. Retrieved 11-10-2010.

Halper, S. 2010. Beijing's coalition of the willing. *Foreign Policy.* July/August. 100-102.

Hartle, D.G. 1983. The Theory of 'rent-seeking': some reflections. *Canadian Journal of Economics.* 16(4), 539-554.

International Development Research Centre (IDRC). Undated. State Sovereignty. www.idrc.ca/en

Ministry of Foreign Affairs of the Peoples Republic of China (MFAPRC). 2004. Shanghai Cooperation Organization. www.fmprc.gov.cn/eng/topics/sco/t57970.htm

Office of the Special Adviser on the Prevention of Genocide (OSAPG), 2009. Prevention of genocide. Booklet on what is genocide, why it happens and what is the role of the Special Adviser of the Secretary General, the United Nations system and the International Criminal Court. UN Department of Public Information / the Office of the Special Adviser on the Prevention of Genocide. February 2009. www.un.org/preventgenocide/adviser .

Oppenheimer, N. 2008. Diamonds, Development and Democracy. *World Policy Journal*. 25 (3), 211-217.

Rawls, J. 1971. *A Theory of Justice*. Harvard University Press, Cambridge, Massachusetts.

Rotberg, R.I. 2010. Mugabe Uber Alles. *Foreign Affairs*. 89 (4), 10-18.

Sieff, M. 2008. Africa: Many Hills to Climb. *World Policy Journal*. 25 (3), 185-195.

CHAPTER 10
MILLENNIUM DEVELOPMENT GOALS I-III: POVERTY AND HUNGER, EDUCATION, AND GENDER PARITY

MILLENNIUM DEVELOPMENT GOALS

Emanating from the Millennium Declaration, the Millennium Development Goals bind countries to do more in the attack on inadequate incomes, widespread hunger, gender inequality, environmental deterioration and lack of education, health care and clean water.

> --UNDP (2003) Human Development Report 2003, *Millennium Development Goals: A Compact among Nations to End Human Poverty.*

The region [Sub-Saharan Africa] is off-track to meet every Millennium Development Goal.

> --UNMP (2005) *Investing in Development: A Practical Plan to Achieve the Millennium Development Goals.*

The current conceptual framework for assisting developing countries is provided by the United Nations Millennium Declaration (UNGA, 2000) which was signed by 189 countries at the September 2000 UN Millennium Summit. The specific objectives of the Declaration are specified in the set of Millennium Development Goals (MDGs). The MDGs echo earlier goals embodied in the results of other meetings such as the 1991 World Health Assembly sponsored by the World Health Organization (WHO), the 1994 International Conference on Population and Development (also known as the Cairo Consensus), the 1996 World Food Summit, and the 2000 World Education Forum (Education for All). The spirit of the MDGs has also been endorsed by the 2001 "Doha Development Agenda" of the World Trade Organization (WTO, 2001), and the 2002 "Monterrey Consensus" (United Nations, 2002). The Millennium Declaration, as the conceptual framework for international development, was reaffirmed by the UN at the 2005 and the 2010 World Summits (UNGA, 2005, 2010), affirmed at the 2005 G8 Gleneagles Summit, and affirmed by the 2009 G20 London Summit.

The following set of eight specific Goals forms the MDGs:

GOAL 1:	Eradicate extreme poverty and hunger
GOAL 2:	Achieve universal primary education
GOAL 3:	Promote gender equality and empower women
GOAL 4:	Reduce child mortality
GOAL 5:	Improve maternal health
GOAL 6:	Combat HIV/AIDS, malaria, and other diseases
GOAL 7:	Ensure environmental sustainability
GOAL 8:	Develop a global partnership for development

Each Goal has at least one target, and each target has at least one indicator/measure. These targets, generally speaking, specify the region's or country's performance outcomes to be achieved by a target date (in most cases, 2015) relative to the respective performance levels in 1990. The year 2010 marked the two-thirds point between the starting date of 2000 and the target date of 2015.

The Millennium Declaration formally recognized the "special needs of Africa" in the development process. As the above quotes show, Africa has struggled with the MDGs for the decade since the Millennium Declaration was signed. Indeed, the 2010 World Summit on the MDGs noted that the membership "recognizes that more attention should be given to Africa, especially those countries most off-track to achieve the Millennium Development Goals by 2015." This chapter examines the MDG performance of Sub- Saharan Africa (SSA) relative to the indicators for other regions of the world. The first seven MDGs and their respective numerical targets will be stated, and available statistical information will be presented and briefly discussed in this chapter. The set of MDGs is used as a vehicle for discussing development issues facing regions of the world.

The MDG framework was employed by Rauch and Kostyshak (2009) in discussing the performance of Arabic countries, by Forster (2010) in a brief assessment of SSA development, and by Forster (2012) in comparing, and contrasting, development in China and India.

POVERTY AND HUNGER

MDG 1: Eradicate Extreme Poverty and Hunger

Of all developing regions, Sub-Saharan Africa alone remains seriously off track to achieve the poverty reduction MDG, and the global economic crisis threatened to interrupt the region's recent progress in picking up the pace on economic growth and poverty reduction.

> --World Bank (2009a). Global Monitoring Report 2009-*A Development Crisis*.

Poverty

Target 1: Halve, between 1990 and 2015, the proportion of people whose income is less than "one dollar a day"

The 2009 World Summit on Food Security, held in Rome, noted with alarm that "the number of people suffering from hunger and poverty now exceeds 1 billion" (FAO, 2009a). In early 2009, the threshold used for extreme poverty was revised from the $1.00 per day (in the stated target) to $1.25 at 2005 PPP (World Bank, 2009a, b). These revisions are incorporated in Table 1. At 57.6 %, SSA had the highest proportion of people living in extreme poverty in 1990. The SSA proportion of people living in extreme poverty decreased in 2005. However, the proportion was still the highest of the regions and remained slightly above half of the population at 50.9 % which was still significantly above the target of 28.8 % for 2015. While the incidence of poverty in SSA decreased by almost 7 %, the number of people in SSA actually living on less than $1.25 per day increased by 92.7 million from 295.7 million in 1990 to 388.4 million in 2005. A larger number of South Asians (579.2 million) were living on less than $1.25 per day in 1990 but the number is higher for 2005 (595.6 million).

Table 1: Proportion and Number of People in Developing Regions Living on Less Than $1.25 per Day

Region	Proportion (%)			Number (millions)		
Year	1990	2005	2015*	1990	2005	2015*
SSA	**57.6**	**50.9**	**38.0**	**295.7**	**388.4**	**366.0**
East Asia & Pacific	54.7	16.8	5.9	873.3	316.2	120.0
Europe & Central Asia	2.0	3.7	1.7	9.1	17.3	7.0
Latin America & Caribbean	11.3	8.2	5.0	49.6	45.1	30.0
Middle East & North Africa	4.3	3.6	1.8	9.7	11.0	6.0
South Asia	51.7	40.3	22.8	579.2	595.6	388

Source: World Bank (2009 a, b; 2010). 2015* figures are estimated based upon the 2010 GMR's post-2008 crisis scenario.

Human Development Indices (HDIs)

Alternative metrics to the "$ income per day" for measuring human well-being have included the Human Development Index (HDI) and the Human Poverty Index for Developing Countries (HPI-1) which have been provided in the UNDP's annual Human Development Reports (HDRs). The HDI measures achievement while the HPI-1 measures deprivation.

The HDI is based upon indices for life expectancy (as an indicator of health), education and per capita income (as an indicator of living standards). The 2007 HDI indices and the 2007 HDI-component indices are provided for developing regions in Table 2.

In Table 2, SSA scores at the bottom for each HDI component index and hence also has the lowest overall HDI rating among the developing regions. The greatest shortfall for SSA is for the life expectancy index.

Commencing with the 2010 Human Development Report, the methodology for computing the HDI's was revised. The education index for 2007 in Table 2 was based upon adult literacy and gross enrollment (all levels combined). In the revised methodology, the education index is based upon the mean years of schooling and the expected years of schooling. Gross National Income (GNI) per capita replaces GNP per capita in the new methodology. The 2010 HDI indices along with their component measures are given in Table 3.

Table 2: Human Development Indicators and Component Indices, 2007

Region	Life Expectancy Index	Education Index	GDP per capita Index	HDI
SSA	**0.441**	**0.597**	**0.503**	**0.514**
Arab States	0.726	0.695	0.736	0.719
East Asia & Pacific	0.786	0.849	0.676	0.770
Latin America & Caribbean	0.806	0.886	0.770	0.821
South Asia	0.651	0.621	0.562	0.612
Central & Eastern Europe And CIS	0.745	0.916	0.802	0.821

Source: UNDP (2009)

Table 3: 2010 HDIs and 2010 HDI Components

Region	Life Expectancy	Mean years of schooling	Expected years Of schooling	GNI per capita PPP 2008 $	HDI
SSA	**52.7**	**4.5**	**9.0**	**2,050**	**0.389**
Arab States	69.1	5.7	10.8	7,861	0.588
East Asia & Pacific	72.6	7.2	11.5	6,403	0.643
Europe & Central Asia	68.5	9.2	13.6	11,462	0.702
Latin America & Caribbean	74.0	7.9	13.7	10,642	0.704
South Asia	65.1	4.6	10.0	3,417	0.516

Source: UNDP (2010)

Starting with HDR 2010, the setting of development categories no longer use predetermined cutoff values for HDIs. Instead, the categories are set according to quartiles. The top quartile will be the countries classified as having Very High Development levels, and these also receive designation as developed countries. Countries in the other three quartiles are termed developing countries.

The HPI-1 was based upon three measures: the probability of not surviving to age 40 and the percentage of children underweight for age (measures of health), the adult literacy rate (a measure of education) and the average of the percentage of the population without access to an improved water source. Since the HPI-1 was a measure of deprivation, low values were better than higher ones.

Income Equity Approaches

The 2010 HDR introduced a new poverty index, the Multidimensional Poverty Index (MPI) which supplants the HPI-1. UNDP (2010) does not report regional MPI measures; however, it does provide a ranking of 169 developing countries. The Low Development category ranges from rank 128 to rank 169. All but six countries in this category (Afghanistan, Bangladesh, Haiti, Myanmar, Nepal and Yemen) are in SSA. Seven SSA countries are in the Medium Development category (Cape Verde, Congo, Gabon, Namibia, Sao Tome, South Africa and Swaziland).

Another approach to analyzing poverty is to consider the distribution of income across income groups within the countries or regions. The extent of income equality/ inequality across income levels can be portrayed through the use of Lorenz curves which show cumulative income shares as income levels increase. For 16 of the 30 SSA countries, the poorest 20% of their population receive less than 5% of the country's income. The poorest 20% in nine countries receive 4% or less, and in five countries they receive 2% or less.

A summary numerical measure of income equality / inequality which is based upon the concept of the Lorenz Curve is the Gini Index, or the Gini Coefficient, which ranges from 0 (perfect equality) to 1 (perfect inequality). Low Gini Indices indicate greater equality in the income distribution. UNDP (2005) provides regional Gini Indices for some regions of the world as well as country-specific indices for several countries. Table 4 lists the Gini coefficients for the UNDP (2005) world regions.

Table 4: Regional Gini Coefficients

Region	SSA	East Asia & Pacific	Latin America & Caribbean	South Asia	Central & Eastern Europe & CIS
Gini Indices	72.2	52	57.1	33.4	42.8

Source: UNDP (2005)

Gini coefficients above 50 are viewed as high income inequality (UNDP, 2005). The SSA has the highest Gini Index indicating it has the highest degree of income inequality among the regions. UNDP (2007) does not list regional Gini estimates; however, it provides a list of 11 SSA countries with Gini Indices over 50 and five over 60. World Bank (2005a) commented that the distribution of income in Africa has become more unequal since 1970 "with the income of the poorest people deteriorating but the income of the richest remaining stable."

The Inequality-Adjusted HDI (IHDI).

In order to account for the losses in human development caused by inequalities in health, in education and in income, the 2010 HDR introduced the inequality-adjusted Human Development Index (IHDI). Information concerning these indices is given in Table 5.

Table 5: 2010 Regional HDIs and 2010 Regional Inequality-Adjusted HDIs (IHDIs) and IHDI Inequality-Adjusted (I-A) Components

Region	HDI	IHDI	% Loss due to inequality	I-A Life-Expectancy Index	I-A Education Index	I-A Income Index
SSA	**0.389**	**0.261**	**33**	**0.294**	**0.254**	**0.238**
Arab States	0.588	0.426	28	0.619	0.289	0.432
East Asia & Pacific	0.643	0.505	21	0.699	0.452	0.407
Europe and Central Asia	0.702	0.607	14	0.672	0.623	0.535
Latin America & Caribbean	0.704	0.527	25	0.728	0.510	0.395
South Asia	0.516	0.361	30	0.499	0.246	0.383

Source: UNDP (2010)

Each region shows a drop in overall well-being due to the effects of inequality with SSA showing the largest drop followed by South Asia. In SSA, inequality results in well-being dropping by one-third.

Hunger

MDG 1, Target 2: Halve, between 1990 and 2015, the proportion of people who suffer from hunger.

The proportion of the SSA population which is undernourished is the highest of any region with almost one-third of the population being undernourished in 2009 and 2010. Since 1990, SSA has made only meager progress on reducing the proportion of its population which suffers from malnutrition.

Table 6: Proportion of Population Undernourished 1990-92 to 2010

Region	1990 - 1992	2000– 2002	2005-2007	2009*	2010*
SSA	**34**	**31**	**28**	**33**	**30**
Near East and North Africa	6	8	8	9	8
Asia & Pacific	20	16	16	18	16
Latin America & Caribbean	12	10	8	9	9

Source: FAO (2010). * Figures are authors' estimates based upon a set of bar charts in FAO

The 1996 World Food Summit's related hunger goal is to halve the number of undernourished people by 2015. Table 7 shows that SSA has the second largest number of undernourished people after Asia & the Pacific.

Table 7: Number of People Undernourished (millions), 1990-92 to 2010

Region	1990-1992	2000-2002	2005-2007	2009*	2010*
SSA	**165**	**202**	**201**	**250**	**239**
Near East and North Africa	20	32	32	37	37
Asia & Pacific	588	532	555	660	578
Latin America and Caribbean	54	51	47	53	53

Source: FAO (2010). * Figures are authors' estimates based upon a set of bar charts in FAO

UNDP (2010) estimates that the 2008 food price increases may have increased the number of undernourished people by about 63 million, and the economic crisis of 2008-2009 may have added another 41 million in 2009 than would otherwise have been the case. The World Bank (2011) in the *Food Price Watch* announced that the global price increase

between June 2010 and January 2011 caused an additional 44 million people to live in poverty.
Undernourishment occurs in a country when the caloric intake falls short of the country's minimum dietary energy requirement (MDER) - the amount of energy necessary for light activity and maintaining the minimum acceptable weight for height (FAO, 2010). MDER varies over time and across countries. In addition to low caloric intake, malnutrition depends upon the composition of a given caloric intake. According to the WHO (2000), protein energy malnutrition (PEM), the most lethal form of malnutrition, accounted for almost half of nutrition-related premature deaths. Twenty-six percent of PEM children live in Africa. Other forms of malnutrition include iodine deficiency disorders (a cause of brain damage), vitamin A deficiency (a cause of blindness for children and pregnant women), iron deficiency (the most common nutritional disorder and the main cause of anemia), and obesity.

Reducing child malnutrition (which plays a major role in about 50% of child deaths annually in developing countries) is also part of the hunger target. Regional indicators of child malnutrition -- prevalence of stunting (low height for age), underweight (low weight for age) and wasting (low weight for height) –based upon national surveys from 1980/92 are given in Table 8. The highest prevalence and the greatest number of children suffering from malnutrition are in Southern Asia. In aggregate terms, de Onis et al. (1993) note that Asia accounts for 80% of malnourished children, Africa accounts for 15%, and the remaining 5% are in Latin America. Within Africa, Eastern Africa accounts for the highest prevalence, and the largest number, of stunted children. For Africa, the highest prevalence of, and number of, underweight and wasted children are in Western Africa. Northern Africa has the lowest prevalence and numbers in all categories.

De Onis et al. (2000) provided updated results for child stunting. Almost one-third of children under age 5 in developing countries were forecast to be stunted in 2000. This amounted to 182 million stunted children of whom 70% lived in Asia, 26% in Africa, and 4% in Latin America and the Caribbean. One hundred and eighty-two million represents a decrease of 40 million stunted children since 1980 as the prevalence rate fell from 47% to slightly less than 33%. The prevalence of stunting in Africa fell from 41% in 1980 to 35.2% in 2000, with North Africa showing a very significant decrease from almost 33% to about 20% over this time period. On the other hand, Eastern Africa had an increase in stunting prevalence from 47% in 1980 to 49% in 2000. While the African prevalence of stunting fell over the 1980-2000 period, the number of stunted children was forecast to grow from 34.8 million to 47.3 million with these increases occurring in eastern Africa (from 12.9 million to 22.0 million) and Western Africa (from 9.0 million to 14.7 million). The number in North Africa decreases from 6.0 million to 4.4 million.

Table 8: Regional Estimates of the Prevalence of, and Number of, Stunted, Underweight and Wasted Children

Region	Stunted %	Stunted Number (millions)	Underweight %	Underweight Number (millions)	Wasted %	Wasted Number (millions)
Western Africa	**37.9**	**14.1**	**32.8**	**12.2**	**9.5**	**3.5**
Eastern Africa	**47.0**	**17.5**	**31.0**	**11.5**	**6.0**	**2.2**
North Africa	**25.4**	**5.5**	**11.3**	**2.4**	**5.8**	**1.2**
Caribbean	25.9	0.9	19.4	0.6	2.2	0.1
Central America	29.8	4.8	17.7	2.8	4.6	0.7
Southern America	18.1	6.4	8.4	2.4	1.9	0.7
Southern Asia	60.3	100.9	60.5	101.2	17.3	28.9
South Eastern Asia	43.2	24.9	37.8	21.8	7.6	4.4
Eastern Asia	32.1	39.2	21.3	26.0	3.6	4.4
Melanesia	42.2	0.3	29.5	0.2	5.5	0.0

Source: de Onis et al. (1993)

de Onis et al. (2004) reported on the prevalence of children underweight in 1990 compared to those estimated for 2015. While the estimates for worldwide prevalence show a decline from 26.5 % in 1990 to 17.8% in 2015, the prevalence for underweight in Africa is predicted to increase from 24.0% to 26.8%. Within Africa, the largest increase in the child underweight prevalence is in Eastern Africa. Middle, Southern and Western Africa are forecast to have decreased prevalence with the largest reduction occurring in Middle Africa (from 27.8% to 23.6%). Twelve African countries had very high levels of child underweight (Angola, Burkina Faso, Burundi, Democratic Republic of the Congo, Eritrea,

Ethiopia, Madagascar, Mali, Mauritania, Niger, Nigeria, and Sudan). Levinson and Bassett (2007) reported that underweight continues to rise in SSA.

The effect of malnutrition on health and mortality may be measured by "Disability –Adjusted Life Years" (DALYs) which is "the sum of years of life lost" due to premature death and disabilities (FAO, 2004). The leading risk factor for DALYs in high mortality developing countries is underweight. According to FAO (2004), underweight accounts for 50% of DALYs lost due to diarrhea, pneumonia, and malaria.

Protracted (Food) Crisis Situations

FAO (2010) describes protracted crises as situations featuring "recurrent natural disasters and/or conflict, longevity of food crises, breakdown of livelihoods and insufficient institutional capacity to react to the crises." Food insecurity is a major manifestation of protracted crisis situations.

FAO (2010) uses three criteria in determining the presence of a protracted crisis:

1. Longevity of the crisis. The country has been on the FAO Global Information and Early Warning System (GIEWS) list for eight years or more during the 2001-2010 period, or 12 years between 1996 and 2010.

2. The proportion of Official Development Assistance (ODA) going to humanitarian aid equals or exceeds 10 percent since 2000.

3. The country in question is on the FAO list of low income food deficit countries (LIFDCs)

FAO (2010) determined that 22 countries meet all three of the criteria as of 2010. Seventeen of the 22 countries are in SSA, and are listed in Table 9.

Somalia and Sudan have humanitarian aid that makes up more than 60% of their total assistance. Seven countries have humanitarian aid equal to or exceeding 30%.

Table 9: SSA Countries Determined to be in Protracted Crisis Situations as of 2010

Country	Total Disasters (1996-2010) Years	Share of Humanitarian Aid In Total ODA (2000-2008) %
Angola	12	30
Burundi	15	32
Cent. Afr. Rep.	8	13
Chad	9	23
Congo	13	22
Cote d'Ivoire	9	15
DR Congo	15	27
Eritrea	15	30
Ethiopia	15	21
Guinea	10	16
Kenya	12	14
Liberia	15	33
Sierra Leone	15	19
Somalia	15	64
Sudan	15	62
Uganda	14	10
Zimbabwe	10	31

Source: FAO (2010)

Global Hunger Index (GHI)

The Global Hunger Index (GHI) is based on equally - weighted indicators:

1. The proportion of people who are undernourished as estimated by FAO.

2. The Prevalence of Underweight in Children under 5 years of age according to WHO.

3. The Under-5 Mortality Rate reported by UNICEF.

Table 10: 2009 GHI and Its Components, and 2010, 2011GHIs, for SSA Countries in Protracted Crises (in 2010)

Country	Proportion of Undernourished 2005-07	Under-5 Underweight For age 2002-07	Under-5 Mortality Rate 2007	Global Hunger Index 2009	Global Hunger Index 2010*	Global Hunger Index 2011*
Angola	41	14.2	15.8	25.3	27.2	24.2
Burundi	62	35	18.0	38.7	38.3	37.9
Cent. Afr. Rep.	40	24.0	17.2	28.1	27.4	27.0
Chad	37	33.9	20.9	31.3	30.9	30.6
Congo	15	11.8	12.5	15.4	15.2	13.2
Cote d'Ivoire	14	16.7	12.7	14.5	14	18.0
DR Congo	69	25.1	16.1	39.1	41	39.0
Eritrea	64	34.5	7.0	36.5	35.7	33.9
Ethiopia	41	34.6	11.9	30.8	29.8	28.7
Guinea	17	22.5	15.0	18.2	17.1	17.3
Kenya	31	16.5	12.1	20.2	19.4	18.6
Liberia	33	20.4	13.3	24.6	24.3	21.5
Sierra Leone	35	28.3	26.2	33.8	28.9	25.2
Somalia	NA	32.8	14.2	NA	NA	NA
Sudan	22	27.0	10.9	19.6	20.9	21.5
Uganda	21	16.4	13.0	14.8	15.0	16.7
Zimbabwe	30	14.0	9.0	21.0	20.9	17.7

Source: FAO (2010). *2010 and 2011 GHI figures are from IFPRI (2010, 2011)

The scores in Table 10 do not reflect the impacts of the famine that struck the Horn of Africa in 2011.

IFPRI categorizes countries according to where the value of their GHIs is placed on the following "rating line":

low moderate serious alarming extremely alarming
1----------5------------10-----------20------------------30

The SSA countries in Table 11 are fairly evenly distributed across the serious to extremely alarming categories according to the 2009 GHI while, for the 2010 GHI, there are two fewer countries (Ethiopia and Sierra Leone) in the extremely alarming category with Ethiopia and Sierra Leone moving down to the alarming category. Also, Kenya and Sudan switched memberships between the serious and alarming groups. GUIs in 2011 place all but one country in the same cell as in 2010. The change is for Zimbabwe improving from Alarming in 2010 to Serious in 2011.

Table 11: State of Food Insecurity for SSA Countries in Protracted Crises

Category	2009 GHI countries	2010 GHI countries	2011 GHI countries
0-4.9 Low	0	0	0
5.0-9.9 Moderate	0	0	0
10-19.9 Serious	Congo, Cote d'Ivoire Guinea, Sudan, Uganda	Congo, Cote d'Ivoire Guinea, Kenya, Uganda	Congo, Cote d'Ivoire Guinea, Kenya, Uganda Zimbabwe
20-29.9 Alarming	Angola, CAR, Kenya Liberia, Zimbabwe	Angola, CAR, Ethiopia, Liberia Sierra Leone, Sudan, Zimbabwe	Angola, CAR, Ethiopia, Liberia Sierra Leone, Sudan
30- Extremely Alarming	Burundi, Chad, DR Congo Eritrea, Ethiopia, Sierra Leone	Burundi, Chad, DR Congo Eritrea	Burundi, Chad, DR Congo Eritrea

Source: FAO (2010) and Table 10

Globally, IFPRI (2010) found 29 countries in either the alarming or extremely alarming groups using the 2010 GHIs. Regional GHIs for 1990, 2010 and 2011 are given in Table 12.

Table 12: Regional GHI Values for 1990, 2010 and 2011

Region	GHI 1990	GHI 2010	2010 Assessment	GHI 2011		2011 Assessment
SSA	**25.3**	**21.7**	**Alarming**	**20.5**		**Alarming**
South Asia	30.7	22.9	Alarming	22.6		Alarming
SE Asia	14.4	8.6	Moderate	8.0		Moderate
Near East & North Africa	7.5	5.1	Moderate	4.8		Low
Latin America & Caribbean	8.7	4.9	Low	4.9		Low

Source: IFPRI (2010, 2011)

FAO (2004) argued that war and civil conflict should be considered as major contributors to short-term food crises and also chronic hunger. FAO (2005) listed 27 SSA countries requiring urgent external [food] assistance. The major causes of the latter situation were: drought (13 countries), civil strife (seven countries), and internally displaced persons (seven countries).

UNDP (2003) commented that "Agricultural output in Sub-Saharan Africa, for instance, has been bedeviled by low productivity, even though high-yielding varieties are available for maize, rice and wheat." According to FAO (2009b), SSA had the highest growth rate of grain production since 1990; however, almost 90% of this growth came from area expansion rather than productivity enhancement. SSA yields at roughly one-third of the global average are the lowest in the world. Improving soil quality is the most pressing need for many farmers in SSA. Further impacting yields, rainfall levels have been decreasing since 1968 and have been subject to wider fluctuations. FAO (2009a) specified "Five Rome Principles for Sustainable Global Food Security." These included:

1. Invest in country-owned plans, aimed at channeling resources to well-designed and results-based programs and partnerships.
2. Foster strategic coordination at national, regional and global level to improve governance, promote better allocation of resources, avoid duplication of efforts and identify response-gaps.
3. Strive for a comprehensive twin-track approach to food security that consists of:
    - Direct action to immediately tackle hunger for the most vulnerable
    - Medium-and long-term sustainable agricultural, food security, nutrition and rural development programs to eliminate the root causes of hunger and poverty, including through the progressive realization of the right to adequate food.
4. Ensure a strong role for the multilateral system by sustained improvements in sufficiency, responsiveness, coordination and effectiveness of multilateral institutions.
5. Ensure sustained and substantial commitment by all partners to investment in agriculture and food security and nutrition, with provision of necessary resources in a timely and reliable fashion, aimed at multi-year plans and programs.

The Copenhagen Consensus (2009), a think tank of economists and scientists, listed combating child malnutrition as the top priority of a set of world problems. According to this group the benefits of a dollar spent on this issue generates 17 dollars in benefits.

EDUCATION

MDG 2: Achieve Universal Primary Education

Target 3: Ensure that, by 2015, children everywhere, boys and girls alike, will be able to complete a full course of primary schooling.

As shown in Table 13, the net primary school enrollment ratios for SSA are the lowest of the developing regions by a considerable margin with only 58% of relevant age children being enrolled in primary school in 1999 and 76% in 2008.

Table 13: Adjusted Net Primary Education Enrollment Ratios, 1999 and 2008

Regions	SSA	CIS, Europe	Western Asia	Southern Asia	CIS, Asia	North Africa	South-eastern Asia	Latin America & Caribbean	Eastern Asia
1999	58	89	83	79	75	86	93	94	95
2008	76	93	88	90	94	94	95	95	96

Source: UN (2010)

The statistics in Table 13 deal with school *enrollments*, but they do not reflect school *completion*. In 50% of the countries in South and West Asia and in SSA about 33% of enrolled children will drop out of school before reaching completion. Many drop out before completing the first grade (UNESCO, 2010a). The 2005 SSA primary school completion rate for females was 55% and 65% for males. These completion rates are the lowest of the developing regions with the next lowest being South Asia with female and male completion rates of 77% and 83% respectively (World Bank, 2009a). UNESCO (2010a) put the SSA situation in stark perspective, "the average 15 year old child in SSA does not attend school."

Table 14: Percent of Children and Adolescents of Primary or Lower Secondary Education Age NOT Enrolled in Primary or Lower Secondary Education, 2007

Region		SSA	South & West Asia	Arab States	Latin America & Caribbean	Central Asia	East Asia & the Pacific	Central and Eastern Europe
Education Level	Primary	26	10	14	5	5	5	7
	Lower Secondary	38	23	18	5	4	10	7

Source: UNESCO (2010a)

SSA and South & West Asia have the highest ratios of children and adolescents of primary or lower secondary education age not enrolled in school with 26% of SSA primary age children not enrolled in primary education, and 38 % of lower secondary age adolescents not being enrolled. The figures for South & West Asia are 10% and 28% respectively. Taken together these two regions have about 100 million students not enrolled in either primary or lower secondary school. Many adolescents who are enrolled in school are still in primary level schools. In SSA, this amounts to 39% of lower secondary age adolescents being enrolled in primary school levels (UNESCO, 2010a).

Factors Impacting Education Quality

There are various additional factors that may inhibit or not enhance educational quality. Large student-teacher ratios in SSA may contribute to the lower quality of education in SSA. The most commonly used international metric for student/teacher is a 40:1 ratio, a figure that is exceeded by 22 SSA countries (UNESCO, 2010b). Table 15 lists the primary pupil –teacher ratios in developing regions for 2000. The 45 % primary pupil-teacher ratio in SSA is significantly higher than those of other developing regions with only South &West Asia's 39% coming close.

Another concern is the shortage of appropriately trained teachers. It is estimated that SSA requires almost an additional million trained teachers (UNESCO, 2011).

Table 15: Primary Pupil-Teacher Ratios, 2008

SSA	East Asia & Pacific	Central Asia	Latin America/ Caribbean	Arab States	South & West Asia	Central & Eastern Europe
45	19	17	23	22	39	18

Source: UNESCO (2011).

The language of instruction is an important input influencing the outcome of the teaching-learning experience process with students performing better when they receive instruction in their native language (UNDP, 2003, 2004). This result is particularly important for Francophone countries in Africa where French is the language of instruction (UNDP, 2003). UNDP (2004) noted that bilingual schools in Africa perform better than monolingual ones. This finding is echoed by UNESCO (2010). Bilingual students in Mali outperformed those taught solely in French. UNDP (2004) also commented that local language is generally used for the first three grades in SSA, but then instruction moves to French, English or Portuguese.

While it appears that there are a very large number of African languages, most of them are dialects of core languages. Seventy-five percent speak one of 12 core languages, and 85% speak one of 15 core languages (UNDP, 2004). These core languages could be used in all grades and perhaps enhance student learning.

Verner (2005) notes that Francophone countries in SSA are characterized by higher illiteracy rates, higher student-teacher ratios, lower primary enrollment ratios, and lower GNP per capita when compared to Anglophone countries. Verner's model indicated that a 10% increase in either enrollment rates or years of schooling yielded literacy rates increases of 2.6% and 3.7% respectively. Finally, Verner found that literacy rates were not affected by location, indicating that literacy rates in Africa were not significantly lower than other developing regions after controlling for other variables. In other words, Verner found no separate "Africa" effect to the results.

Kramer and Moulin (2009) found that providing textbooks, another educational input, did not raise average test scores (an outcome measure of learning) except for the best students (measured by pre-test scores). This result is in contrast to an evaluation of Ghana's education which credited increased availability of textbooks "in part" with improvements in mathematics and English test scores from 1998 to 2003 (UNESCO, 2010b).

HIV/Aids may affect both the demand for education and the supply of a given quality of education in high prevalence countries. As children lose one or both parents to HIV/AIDS, it may become excessively burdensome to send children to school. The impact may be more severe for females who are then needed for household labor. HIV/AIDS also takes a toll on teachers and consequently on the quality of their work and learning outcomes.

Another factor degrading the educational experience which is seldom acknowledged is quiet corruption. Examples include non-illness- related teacher absences and low effort while on the job.

UNESCO (2011) asserted that "violent conflict is still one of the greatest obstacles to accelerated progress in education." Using established criteria, UNESCO identified a set of 35 countries that experienced armed conflict during 1999-2009. In this set there are 30 low income and lower middle income countries. The "conflict group of 30" (CG-30) has the following characteristics:

- 116 million children
- 28 million primary school age children out of school
- Survival rate to last grade is 65% compared to 86% in non-conflict poor countries
- Secondary school gross enrollment ratio of 48% compared to 67% in non-conflict countries
- Youth literacy rate of 79% and adult literacy rate of 69% compared to 93% and 85% respectively in non-conflict countries.

Thirteen of the CG-30 are SSA countries. Table 16 shows the conflict costs to education, in terms of years of schooling lost, for four selected SSA countries along with their respective time periods of conflict.

Table 16: Education Years Lost Due to Conflict in Selected SSA Countries

Country	Conflict Period	Avg. years of Education at start of conflict	Years of schooling lost
Burundi	1978-2001	2.9	3.4
Mozambique	1977-1992	2.7	5.3
Rwanda	1990-1994	4.9	1.2
Somalia	1986-1996	2.9	2.3

Source: UNESCO (2011)

Literacy

Even high school enrollments and completion do not ensure high quality educational outcomes. Bennell (2002), in discussing problems in achieving universal primary education (UPE) in SSA, indicated that 60% of SSA students in his study were functionally illiterate when they leave school due to low quality of education. Achieving a 50% improvement in the levels of youth and adult literacy is part of Goals 3 and 4 of the 2000 World Education Summit's Dakar Framework for Action (UNESCO, 2010). Repetition rates are very high in the majority of countries, and these rates are indicators of low quality of education. Another sign of poor quality education in SSA is the fact that, in 21 countries, 22-24 year olds with five years of education had a 40% chance of being illiterate.

Bennell (2002) notes that poor people need to believe that education significantly improves their children's chances of gaining better jobs if they are to invest in education. In support of this intuition, Hanushek and Woessmann (2008) concluded that cognitive skill development is the key issue in the impact of schooling on economic well-being.

Table 17: Adult and Youth Illiteracy Rates, 2005-2008*

Region	Adult illiteracy rate (% aged 15 and over)	Youth illiteracy rate (% aged 15-24)
SSA	**38**	**29**
South and West Asia	38	21
Arab States	28	13
Latin America And Caribbean	9	3
Central Asia	1	0
East Asia and the Pacific	6	2
Central and Eastern Europe	2	1

Source: Derived from UNESCO (2011).
*Most recent year in the interval.

It seems natural that technical and vocational education (TVE) would be of high value in obtaining jobs in developing countries. Goal 3 of the Dakar Framework for Action deals with ensuring "equitable access to appropriate learning and life-skills programmes" (UNESCO, 2010a). However, TVE has a stigma in some developing countries. It is seen as a safety net for failing students and those from poor families. TVE enrollments are smaller than for secondary school. Table 18 provides enrollment shares for TVE in secondary education.

Table 18: Enrollment Shares for TVE in Secondary Education 2008

Region	**SSA**	**South & West Asia**	**Arab States**	**Latin America & Caribbean**	**Central Asia**	**East Asia & Pacific**	**Central & Eastern Europe**
TVE Share of Secondary Enrollment	7	1	13	11	15	16	19

Source: UNESCO (2011)

South &West Asia and SSA had the lowest shares of secondary enrollment in TVE with 1% and 7%, respectively. In both developed and developing countries, TVE is relatively expensive to provide. For the OECD, TVE is about 15 % higher than general education. In SSA, it may be up to 14 *times* as expensive.

GENDER EQUALITY

MDG 3: Promote Gender Equality and Empower Women

If only I can get educated, I will surely be the President.

--Teenager in rural Malawi, Gibbs (2011)

Table 19 provides some specifics concerning gender inequities.

Table 19: Gender Inequality Indices and Their Respective Components

Regions	Gender Inequality Index 2008	Labor market		Empowerment			Reproductive health	
		Labor Force Participation % 2008		Population with at least Secondary Education % 2010		Parliamentary Seats % F 2008	Adolescent Fertility Rate [a,c] 1990-2008[d]	Maternal Mortality Ratio [b,c] 2003-2008[d]
		F	M	F	M			
SSA	0.735	63.8	82.3	23.9	38.1	17.3	122.3	881
Arab States	0.699	27.0	78.2	31.8	45.0	8.7	42.6	238
East Asia & The Pacific	0.467	70.1	84.5	48.2	61.4	19.8	18.1	126
Europe and Central Asia	0.498	58.6	75.0	78.0	74.0	12.5	28.2	41
Latin America & The Caribbean	0.609	55.3	83.3	51.3	52.7	17.5	72.6	122
South Asia	0.739	37.2	84.2	27.4	49.1	10.4	65.0	454

a) number of live births per 1,000 females aged 15-19, **b)** maternal deaths per 100,000 live births, **c)** these concepts are discussed below, **d)** most recent date available within the time period

Source: UNDP (2010)

SSA and South Asia are virtually tied for the largest Gender Inequality Index. The female participation rate is highest in East Asia & the Pacific followed by SSA. SSA has the highest Adolescent Fertility rate, and it also has the highest Maternal Mortality ratio (the latter concept will be explained in the section dealing with maternal health).

Target 4: Eliminate gender disparity in primary and secondary education preferably by 2005, and in all levels of education no later than 2015

Primary and secondary school girl/boy enrollment ratios in 2008 are lowest in SSA, Oceania and Western Asia. These regions did not satisfy the gender parity goal in "primary and secondary education… by 2005" target of MDG 3, Target 4, and are off-track to satisfy the second part dealing with "all levels of education…2015" as well.

Table 20: School Enrollments, Girls per 100 Boys, by School Level and by Region for 1999 and 2008

	Primary			**Secondary**			**Tertiary**	
Regions	**1999**	**2008**		**1999**	**2008**		**1999**	**2008**
SSA	**85**	**91**		**83**	**86**		**71**	**67**
Northern Africa	90	94		93	98		74	95
Western Asia	87	92		76	86		74	95
Southern Asia	84	96		75	87		65	76
South-Eastern Asia	96	97		95	103		95	107
Eastern Asia	101	104		95	105		66	100
CIS	99	99		101	98		121	130
Latin America and Caribbean	97	97		107	108		115	125
Oceania	91	89		89	87		81	84

Source: UN (2010)

At the tertiary level Southern Asia and SSA have the lowest 2008 ratios of females to males, with ratios of 76 and 67 percent respectively.

Seventy-three percent of the global adult literacy gap is accounted for by SSA and South and West Asia, and about two-thirds of the total is made up of women (UNESCO, 2011).

Table 21: Gender Parity Indices (GPI) for Youth (15-24) Literacy and Adult (15+) Literacy, 2005-2008*

Region	Adult GPI F/M	Youth GPI F/M
SSA	**.75**	**.87**
Arab States	.78	.92
Central Asia	1.00	1.00
East Asia & Pacific	.94	1.00
Latin America & Caribbean	0.98	1.01
South & West Asia	.70	.86
Central & Eastern Europe	0.97	.99

Source: UNESCO (2011) * Most recent year in the interval

The SSA youth literacy GPI rate is essentially the same as that of South and West Asia but is lower than the Arab States. The youth GPIs are higher than the adult GPIs for all regions.

Verner (2005) noted that female illiteracy is quite high in some SSA countries. For example, in 2002, over 90% of adult females in Burkina Faso and Niger were illiterate, and 85% of female youths in these countries were illiterate.

Gender Inequality Index (GII)

Another measure of gender equality is provided by the Gender-related Development Index (GDI) presented in the HDRs from 1995 until the 2009 edition. The GDI was based upon female and male life expectancy at birth, male and female adult literacy and male and female earnings. In the UNDP (2009) ranking of 155 country GDIs, SSA accounted for 39 of the lowest 50 GDI scores.

UNDP (2010) replaced the GDI with a new index, the Gender Inequality Index (GII), which reflects gender disparities in reproductive health, empowerment, and labor market participation.

Table 22: The 2008 Gender Inequality Index and Key Components

Region	GII	Maternal mortality ratio	Adolescent fertility rate	Seats in Parliament Female %	Population with at least secondary education Female %	Labor force participation Female %
SSA	**0.735**	**881**	**122.3**	**17.3**	**23.9**	**63.8**
South Asia	0.739	454	65.0	10.4	27.4	37.2
Arab States	0.699	238	42.6	8.7	31.8	27.0
Latin America &Caribbean	0.609	122	72.6	17.5	51.3	55.3
Europe and Central Asia	0.498	41	28.2	12.5	78	58.6
East Asia and The Pacific	0.467	126	18.1	19.8	48.2	70.1

Source: UNDP (2010)

UNESCO (2010) produced a gender specific EFA index (GEI). The GEI is a simple, equally weighted, average of the gender parity indices (GPIs) for primary and secondary school enrollment and the GPI for adult literacy. The GEI combined with the primary adjusted enrollment ratio, the adult literacy, and the survival rate to grade 5 as a measure of the quality of education produces the Education for All Development Index (EDI). The distribution of the number of countries within regions across the EDI values is given in Table 23.

SSA countries score only in the bottom two levels, with two-thirds scoring in the bottom level. The total set of countries also appears to be heavily weighted towards the bottom two levels. However, this is misleading due to the influence of SSA. Netting out the SSA, the Total-Minus SSA gives a different picture. Now the Table reveals that as many countries score in the top two levels as score in the bottom two levels.

The run up in commodity prices between 2003/05 and 2007 has been blamed for increasing the number of people living with hunger. FAO (2008) estimates the number of undernourished people in SSA to have increased by 43 million. While the number of undernourished people in SSA increased, the proportion of undernourished people decreased from 34 to 30 percent. World Bank (2009b) suggests that the run up in food and oil prices "may have increased the number of people living in extreme poverty by between 130 and 150 million." The impact of the world -wide financial, and economic, crises that started in mid-2008 needs to be assessed. This will take time to see if the effects are transitory or whether the crises will have long term repercussion for SSA economic growth performance.

Table 23: The Number of Countries in EDI Groups

Region	Far from EFA EDI<0.8	Intermediate Position 0.8<EDI<0.94	Close to EFA 0.95<EDI<0.96	EFA Achieved 0.97<EDI<1.00	Subtotal sample
SSA	**17**	**8**	**0**	**0**	**25**
Arab States	5	6	3	0	14
Central Asia	0	1	2	5	8
East Asia & The Pacific	2	4	2	4	12
South and West Asia	5	0	1	0	6
Latin America & The Caribbean	1	16	5	4	26
Central and Eastern Europe	0	1	4	11	16
Total	30	36	17	24	107
Total –Minus SSA	13	28	17	25	82

Source: UNESCO (2010a)

REFERENCES

Bennell, P. 2002. Hitting the target: doubling primary school enrollments in Sub-Saharan Africa by 2015. *World Development*. 30(7) 1179-94.

Copenhagen Consensus. 2009. The Results: Copenhagen Consensus Meeting, 2008. www.Copenhagenconsensus.com

De Onis, M., Blossner, M., Borghi, E., Frongillo, E.A., & Morris, R. 2004. Estimates of global prevalence of childhood underweight in 1990 and 2015. Journal of the American Medical Association. 291(21), 2600-2606.

De Onis, M., Frongillo, E.A., & Blossner, M. 2000. Is malnutrition declining? An analysis of changes in levels of child nutrition since 1980. *The Bulletin of the World Health Organization*. 78(10), 1222-1233.

De Onis, M., Monteiro, C., Akre, J., & Clugston, G. 1993. The worldwide magnitude of protein-energy malnutrition: an overview from the WHO global database on child growth. *Bulletin of the World Health Organization*. 71(6), 703-712.

Food and Agriculture Organization (FAO) of the United Nations. 2004. The State of Food Insecurity in the World 2004. Rome, Italy.

Food and Agriculture Organization (FAO) of the United Nations. 2009a. Declaration of the World Summit on Food Security. November, 2009.

Food and Agriculture Organization (FAO) of the United Nations. 2009b. The State of Food Insecurity in the World 2009. Rome, Italy.

Food and Agriculture Organization (FAO) of the United Nations. 2010. The State of Food Insecurity in the World 2010. Rome, Italy.

Forster, B.A. 2010. A Survey of Economic and Human Development Performance Indicators for Sub-Saharan Africa. *International Journal of Business and Economics*. 10(1) 82-93.

Forster, B. A. 2012. Human and Economic Development in China and India: A Comparative MDG Assessment. *Journal of Applied Business and Economics*, forthcoming.13(2)

Hanushek, E.A., & Woessmann, L. 2008. The role of cognitive skills in economic development. *Journal of Economic Literature*. 46(3) 607-668.

International Food Policy Research Institute (IFPRI). 2010. The Challenge of Hunger: Focus on the Crisis of Child Nutrition. 2010 Global Hunger Index.

International Food Policy Research Institute (IFPRI). 2011. The Challenge of Hunger: Taming Price Spikes and Excessive Food Price Stability. 2011 Global Hunger Index.

Gibbs, N. 2011. The Best Investment. If you really want to fight poverty, fuel growth,
and combat extremism, try girl power. *Time* 2-14-2011. p.64.

Kramer, M., & Moulin, S. 2009. Many children left behind? Textbooks and text scores in Kenya. *AEA Applied Economics*. 1(1), 112-135.

Levinson, F.J. & Bassett, L. 2007. Malnutrition is still a major contributor to child deaths. Population Reference Bureau.

Rauch, J.E. & Kostyshak, S. 2009. The three Arab worlds. *The Journal of Economic Perspectives*. 23(3) 165-188.

United Nations (UN). 2002. Report on the International Conference on Financing for Development. (the Monterrey Consensus), New York, NY.

United Nations (UN). 2010. The Millennium Development Goals Report, 2010. New York, NY

United Nations Development Program (UNDP). 2003. Millennium Development Goals: A Compact Among Nations to End Human Poverty. *Human Development Report* (HDR) 2003. New York, NY.

United Nations Development Program (UNDP). 2004. Cultural Liberty in Today's Diverse World. *Human Development Report* (HDR) 2004. New York, NY.

United Nations Development Program (UNDP). 2005. International Cooperation at a Crossroad: Aid, Trade and Security in an Unequal World. *Human Development Report* (HDR) 2005, New York, NY.

United Nations Development Program (UNDP). 2007. Fighting Climate Change: Human Solidarity in a Divided World. *Human Development Report* (HDR) 2007/2008. New York, NY.

United Nations Development Program (UNDP). 2009. Overcoming Barriers: Human Mobility and Development, *Human Development Report* (HDR). New York, NY.

United Nations Development Program (UNDP). 2010. The Real Wealth of Nations; Pathways to Human Development. *Human Development Report* (HDR). New York, NY.

UNESCO. 2010a. Reaching the marginalized. *Education for All Global Monitoring Report 2010*. Paris, France.

UNESCO. 2010b. Reaching the marginalized. *Education for All Global Monitoring Report 2010.* Regional overview: Sub-Saharan Africa. Paris, France

UNESCO. 2011. The Hidden Crisis: Armed conflict and education. *Education for All Global Monitoring Report, 2011*. Paris, France.

United Nations General Assembly (UNGA). 2005. United Nations 2005 World Summit Outcome. New York, NY.

United Nations General Assembly (UNGA). 2010. Keeping the Promise: United to Achieve the Millennium Development Goals. New York, NY.

United Nations Millennium Project (UNMP). 2005. Investing in Development: A Practical Plan to Achieve the Millennium Development Goals (the Sachs Report). New York, NY.

Verner, D. 2005. What factors influence world literacy? Is Africa different? World Bank Research Working Paper 3496. Washington, DC.

World Bank. 2009a. *Global Monitoring Report 2009: A Development Emergency*. Washington, DC

World Bank. 2009b. *Global Economic Prospects: Commodities at the Crossroads*. Washington, DC.

World Bank. 2011. Food Price Watch. February 2011. Washington, DC.

World Trade Organization (WTO). 2001. Ministerial Declaration. (the Doha Development Agenda). Geneva, Switzerland.

CHAPTER 11
MILLENNIUM DEVELOPMENT GOALS IV-VII: CHILD AND MATERNAL MORTALITY, HIV/AIDS, MALARIA, AND OTHER DISEASES

CHILD MORTALITY AND MATERNAL HEALTH

We are also deeply concerned about the alarming global levels of maternal and child mortality

--The 2010 UN World Summit (UNGA, 2010)

Child Mortality

MDG 4: Reduce Child Mortality

Target 5: Reduce, by two-thirds, between 1990 and 2015, the under-five Mortality Rate.

According to WHO (2005a), there were about 136 million births each year, of which 3.3 million babies were stillborn, another 4.0 or more died within the first 28 days after birth, and 6.6 million children died before their fifth birthday. Over 80% of child deaths occur in Africa and Southern Asia with five countries (China, the Democratic Republic of the Congo, India, Nigeria and Pakistan) accounting for about 50% (UNICEF, 2010).

In 2009, there were 8.1 million under-5 (U_5) deaths globally. For at least three decades the highest average under-five Mortality Rates (U_5MR) in the regions of the world have been those in SSA.

Table 1: Regional U_5MRs (Deaths per 1000 Live Births), 1990 and 2009, MDG 4 Progress, and Regional Total Deaths and Shares of Global U_5 Deaths, 2009

Region	U_5MR 1990	U_5MR 2009	U_5MR 2015 Target	On Track? Y/N	U_5 Deaths 2009	Share of under-five deaths
SSA	**180**	**129**	**60**	**N**	**3,976**	**49.2**
Southern Asia	122	69	41	N	2,677	33.1
Oceania	76	59	25	N	15	0.2
South East Asia	73	36	24	Y	405	5.0
West Asia	66	31	22	Y	159	2.0
North Africa	80	26	27	Y	96	1.2
Latin America & Caribbean	52	23	17	Y	239	3.0
East Asia	45	19	15	Y	361	4.5
CIS	46	23	15	Y		1.1
Developing Regions	99	66	33	N	71	98
World	89	60	30	N		100

Source: UNICEF (2010). MDG Regions

The U_5MRs fell for all regions between 1990 and 2009. The 2009 SSA under-five mortality rate (129) was almost double that of the second-highest region, Southern Asia (69). SSA accounted for almost 50% of total under-five child deaths, and Southern Asia accounted for one-third of the global total. SSA, South Asia and Oceania are not on-track to achieve the MDG concerning U_5MR (UNICEF, 2010).

Globally, pneumonia is the largest single cause of child mortality, accounting for 18% of cases. The next highest cause is diarrhoel disease (15%) followed by pre-term births (12%).

Forty-one percent of under- five deaths are accounted for by neo-natal causes, and 70 % of the deaths occur within the first year of life (UNICEF, 2010). Forty percent of U_5 deaths occurred within the first month of life.

Table 2: Global Causes of Child (U_5) Mortality, 2009 (%)

Cause	**%**
Pneumonia	**18**
Diarrhoel Disease	**15**
Pre-term birth Complications	12
Birth Asphyxia	9
Malaria	8
Sepsis (Neo-natal)	6
Injuries	3
Aids	2
Measles	1
Other Neo-natal	9
All other	16

Source: UNICEF (2010)

Africa accounts for 44% of infant deaths, and South-East Asia accounts for another 36%. There are 31 countries with under-five mortality rates in excess of 100. According to UNICEF (2010), 30 of the 31 are in SSA with child mortality rates ranging from 103 in Gambia to 209 in Chad (the non-SSA country is Afghanistan with a rate of 199). African women currently face a lifetime risk of 1 in 8 of losing a baby before age 5, compared to a risk of 1 in 167 in developed countries (UNICEF, 2010).

SSA also had the highest infant mortality rates (IMRs) for 1990 and 2009. According to UNICEF (2010), in 2009, there were 9 countries with IMR's over 100, and 8 of these were in SSA with IMRs ranging from 101 in Burundi and Mali to 126 in D.R. Congo (again, the other country is Afghanistan with an IMR of 134).

Table 3: Infant Mortality Rates (Infant Deaths per 1000 Live Births), 1990 and 2009

Region	SSA	Southern Asia	Oceania	North Africa	Western Asia	East Asia	South East Asia	Latin America & Caribbean	CIS Asia	CIS Europe
1990	109	87	56	61	52	36	50	41	64	22
2009	81	53	45	23	26	16	29	19	33	12

Source: UNICEF (2010)

Infant mortality rates in all regions decreased between 1990 and 2009; however, they remain highest in SSA. South Asia has the second highest rates in both years. The causes of infant mortality are different from those of child mortality with prematurity, severe infection and asphyxia being the three largest causes of infant mortality.

Maternal Health

MDG 5: Improve Maternal Health

We express grave concern over the slow progress being made in reducing maternal mortality and improving maternal and reproductive health.

--UNGA (2010)

Target 6: Reduce, by three-quarters, between 1990 and 2015, the maternal mortality ratio

According to WHO (2010), about 358,000 women died in 2008 due to maternal causes. WHO defines maternal death as:

> the death of a woman while pregnant or within 42 days of termination of pregnancy, irrespective of the duration and site of the pregnancy, from any cause related to or aggravated by the pregnancy or its management but not from accidental or incidental causes. (WHO, 2010)

The Maternal Mortality Ratio (MMR) is defined as the number of maternal deaths per 100,000 live births during a specified time period.

The Maternal Mortality Rate (MMRate) is the number of maternal deaths in a given period per 100,000 women of reproductive age in that time period. Note MDG 5, Target 6 uses the MMR.

The lifetime risk of maternal death is the probability of dying from a maternal cause during a woman's reproductive lifespan.

Regional MMRs for 1990 and 2008, and the lifetime risk of maternal death in 2008 are given in Table 4.

Table 4: Regional MMRs and Life-Time Risks of Maternal Death

Region	MMR 1990	MMR 2008	Life-time risk of Maternal Death, 1 in:
SSA	**870**	**640**	**31**
Middle East & North Africa	270	170	190
Latin America & Caribbean	140	85	480
South Asia	610	290	110
East Asia & Pacific	200	88	600
Central & Eastern Europe & CIS	69	34	1700
Industrialized Countries	12	14	4300
World	400	260	140

Source: WHO (2010)

MMR's fell between 1990 and 2008 in all regions covered in Table 4. The 2008 SSA incidence of maternal deaths (640) is significantly higher than that of the next highest region, South Asia (290), almost four times that of the Middle East and North Africa and almost eight times that of Latin America and the Caribbean. The lifetime risk of dying for maternal causes is highest for a SSA woman at 1 in 31. In industrialized countries, the risk is 1 in 4300.

Table 5: Global Causes of Maternal Deaths 1997/2007

Cause	%
Hemorrhage	35
Hyper-tension	18
Indirect causes	18
Other Direct causes	11
Abortion & Miscarriage	9
Sepsis	8
Embolism	1

Source: UN (2010)

Target 7: Achieve by 2015, universal access to reproductive health

The proportion of women attending a skilled health care professional rose from 1990 to 2008 in all regions listed below:

Table 6: Proportion (%) of Pregnant Women Attending a Skilled Health-Care Person At Least Once

Region	SSA	Southern Asia	North Africa	Western Asia	Eastern Asia	South-East Asia	Latin America and Caribbean	CIS, Asia
1990	67	48	46	53	80	72	79	90
2008	76	70	78	79	91	93	94	96

Source: UN (2010)

Proportions in all regions increased from 1990 to 2008. Southern Asia fell from second lowest place to the lowest place. SSA has the second lowest proportion of women seeking skilled assistance in 2008.

Table 7: Proportion of Deliveries Attended by a Skilled Health Care Person

Region	SSA	Southern Asia	Oceania	North Africa	Western Asia	Eastern Asia	Southeast Asia	Latin America & Caribbean	CIS
1990	41	30	54	46	62	94	46	72	97
2008	46	45	57	80	78	98	75	86	98

Source: UN (2010)

Table 8: Urban/Rural Ratios for Pregnant Women Using Skilled Care During Childbirth

Region	SSA	Southern Asia	Oceania	North Africa	Western Asia	Eastern Asia	South-East Asia	Latin America & Caribbean	CIS Asia
1990	2.3	2.9	2.0	2.5	1.9	1.0	1.8	1.8	1.1
2008	2.2	2.0	1.9	2.5	1.6	1.0	1.2	1.5	1.0

Source: UN (2010)

Urban/rural ratios have decreased in all regions. North Africa has the highest ratio followed by SSA and Southern Asia. CIS Asia and Eastern Asia have achieved parity between urban and rural populations.

Table 9: Number of Births per 1000 Women Aged 15-19

Region	SSA	Southern Asia	Oceania	North Africa	Western Asia	Eastern Asia	Southeast Asia	Latin America & Caribbean	CIS
1990	124	89	63	43	62	15	53	91	52
2007	121	53	61	31	53	5	44	74	29

Source: UN (2010)

SSA has the highest rate of teenage pregnancy and has shown very little improvement. Latin America and the Caribbean have the second highest rate. Eastern Asia has the lowest rates. The births to teenagers in a set of 24 SSA countries tend to be from rural settings and from the poorest and least educated adolescents (UN, 2010).

Table 10: Proportion of Women Aged 15-49, Married or in a Union, Using any Method of Contraception

Region	SSA	South-ern Asia	Oceania	North Africa	Western Asia	Eastern Asia	Southeast Asia	Latin America & Caribbean	CIS
1990	12	40	28	44	46	78	48	62	61
2007	22	54	28	60	55	86	62	72	70

Source: UN (2010)

SSA had the lowest proportion of women using some method of contraception followed by Oceania. The prevalence of contraceptive use in both regions is roughly 50 % of the use rates of the next closest regions.

HIV/AIDS, MALARIA, AND OTHER DISEASES

MDG 6: Combat HIV/AIDS, Malaria, and Other Diseases

HIV/AIDS

Target 8: Have halted by 2015 and begun to reverse the spread of HIV/AIDS

We have halted and begun to reverse the epidemic. Fewer people are becoming infected with HIV and fewer people are dying from AIDS.

--UNAIDS (2010)

Over the known history of the AIDS/HIV epidemic up until 2007, HIV-related causes were responsible for a total of 25 million deaths (UNAIDS, 2009a).

Table 11: The Number of People Living With HIV, the Number of Newly Infected Adults, the Number of Deaths from AIDS-Related Causes

	Adults and children living with HIV		Adults and children newly infected	AIDS-related deaths of adults and children	
Regions	2001 (millions)	2009 (millions)	2009 (millions)	2001 (millions)	2009 (millions)
SSA	**20.3**	**22.5**	**1.80**	**1.40**	**1.30**
East Asia	0.35	0.77	0.08	0.02	0.04
Oceania	0.03	0.06	0.005	0.001	0.001
South and Southeast Asia	3.8	4.1	0.27	0.23	0.26
Eastern Europe & Central Asia	0.76	1.40	0.13	0.02	0.08
Western & Central Europe	0.63	0.82	0.03	0.007	0.009
Global	28.6	33.3	2.6	1.8	1.8

Source: UNAIDS (2010). *Denotes lower bound estimate.

Globally in 2009, there were 33.3 million people living with HIV, AIDS resulted in the deaths of 1.8 million people. Sixty-eight percent (22.5

million) were living with HIV in SSA. Globally, AIDS deaths peaked at 2.2 million in 2004 (UNAIDS, 2009a). In 2009, AIDS resulted in the deaths of 1.8 million people globally, with 1.3 million (72%) of these being in SSA (UNAIDS, 2010). Globally, women accounted for about 54% of HIV cases while in the SSA almost 60% were female. New HIV infections peaked at 3.5 million in 1996, and in 2009 there were 2.6 million new infections.

The Heads of State of member countries in the African Union met in Abuja, Nigeria in late April 2001 to address the combined threats of HIV/AIDS, Tuberculosis, and Other Related Infectious Diseases for Africa. In mid-2001, the UN General Assembly adopted the (Abuja) Declaration of Commitment on HIV/AIDS (UNGA, 2001).

The Abuja Declaration recognized the special vulnerability of women and girls to HIV, and the UNAIDS (2009b) progress report on HIV/AIDS noted that women are more physiologically susceptible than men to infection during heterosexual intercourse, and this is due to a host of economic, social and legal disadvantages with which women contend and increase their vulnerability to infection. Women and girls in SSA are affected disproportionately by HIV. In the hardest hit regions in SSA young women are about three times more likely to become infected than males.

In 2003, WHO and UNAIDS initiated a program to have 3 million HIV-infected people by 2005 receiving antiretroviral therapy (ART). Under this "3 by 5 program," the number of people in SSA receiving ART doubled from 150,000 to 300,000 in the last 6 months of 2004 (WHO, 2005b). Despite the success with the program, the target proved to be too ambitious.

A new target for MDG 6 is to "Achieve, by 2010, universal access to treatment for HIV/AIDS for all who need it." Since this target is for universal coverage, this target became known as the "All by 2010" program. In practical terms, universal coverage means that 80% of the target population is covered. Estimates suggest that at least 10 million people would need treatment under this criterion, and hence the program is also known as the "10 by 10" program.

MALARIA AND OTHER MAJOR DISEASES

Target 9: Have halted by 2015 and begun to reverse the incidence of malaria and other major diseases

Malaria

In 2009, malaria caused an estimated 225 million episodes of malaria and almost 781 thousand deaths. Ninety-one percent of malaria deaths occurred in Africa, and 85% were children under 5 years of age (WHO, 2010b). SSA by far has the highest risk of malaria. Five countries, Nigeria, the Democratic Republic of the Congo, Ethiopia, Tanzania and Kenya accounted for more than 50% of the SSA cases.

The SSA malaria infections are caused by the following four types of parasites: *Plasmodium falciparum, Plasmodium vivax, Plasmodium malariae, and Plasmodium ovale* (WHO, 2009a). The most common species are *Plasmodium falciparum* and *Plasmodium vivax*, but *Plasmodium falciparum* was "among the leading causes of death worldwide from a single infectious agent in 2004" (WHO, 2008). The SSA region has the most efficient and deadly species of mosquitoes (*Anopheles gambiae*) transmitting the disease. Ninety-eight percent of cases in SSA are estimated to be *Plasmodium falciparum* (RBMP, 2008).

Malaria is a major cause of perinatal mortality, low birth weight and maternal anemia. Ten to 20% of the half-million African children who develop cerebral malaria each year die while another 7% have permanent neurological damage.

On April 25, 2000, representatives from 44 African countries met in Abuja, Nigeria for the "African Summit on Roll Back Malaria," and committed to the goal of cutting malaria mortality in Africa in half by 2010. They also identified the following specific targets to be achieved by 2005:

- At least 60% of those suffering from malaria have prompt access to, and are able to correctly use, affordable and appropriate treatment within 24 hours of the onset of symptoms

- At least 60% of those at risk of malaria, particularly children under five years of age and pregnant women, and benefit from the most suitable combination of personal and community protective measures such as insecticide treated mosquito nets and other interventions which are accessible and affordable to prevent infection and suffering, and

- At least 60% of all pregnant women who at risk of malaria, especially those in their first pregnancies, have access to chemoprophylaxis, or presumptive intermittent treatment. (RBM/WHO, 2003)

In April, 2005, the World Bank announced a new "Booster Program for Malaria" control noting, that while its own efforts were useful, they were "not sufficient for success on a larger scale" (World Bank, 2005a). The World Bank commented that "despite successes in a few countries, measurable progress in malaria control is well below the Abuja 60% coverage targets set by countries and development agencies for 2005 in terms of coverage with preventive and curative interventions." The report mentions that malaria affects other MDGs such as those dealing with education, child mortality and maternal health (MDGs 2, 4 and 5).

RBMP (2008) set forth the following set of ambitious malaria targets in its Global Malaria Action Plan (GMAP):

- *Achieve* **universal coverage**...for all populations at risk with locally appropriate interventions for prevention and case management by 20 and sustain universal coverage until local field research suggests that coverage can gradually be targeted to high risk areas and seasons only, without risk of a generalized resurgence;

- *Reduce* global malaria **cases** from 2000 levels by 50% in 2010 and by 75% by 2015;

- *Reduce* global **deaths** from 2000 levels by 50% in 2010 and to near zero preventable deaths in 2015;

- *Eliminate* malaria in 8-10 countries by 2015 and afterwards in all countries in the pre-elimination phase today; and

- In the long term, *eradicate* malaria world-wide by reducing the global incidence to zero through progressive elimination in countries.

WHO (2005a) observed that about 50% of African children with fever were treated with an anti-malarial drug; however, the treatment uses drugs for which the Plasmodium falciparum parasite has high resistance. Artemisinin-based combination therapies (ACTs) are most effective against Plasmodium falciparum, but these are 10 to 20 times more expensive.

From 2000 to 2010, 33 million malaria tents were purchased and/or distributed (World Bank, 2011). In mid-2010, WHO (2010b) indicates that 42% of African households owned at least one insecticide treated mosquito net (ITN), however, only 35% of children slept under an ITN (WHO, 2008). Hoffmann's (2009) study of Uganda found that despite the knowledge regarding the importance of using ITNs to protect children, the ITNs tended to be used by adults—especially the one who acquired the net. Only when there are sufficient ITNs for all household members will those at higher risk be allocated a net. From 2000-2010, 33 million malaria tents were purchased for distribution (World Bank, 2011). Interior residual spraying (IRS) is "one of the main interventions for reducing and interrupting malaria transmission…" (WHO, 2010b).

Table 12: The Number of Confirmed Malaria Cases and Malaria Deaths, 2000, 2005 and 2009

Regions	Number of confirmed cases (million)			Number of deaths (thousands)		
	2000	2005	2009	2000	2005	2009
Africa	173	188	176	900	853	709
Americas	2.8	1.9	1.1	2.4	1.6	1.3
Eastern Mediterranean	15	12	12	18	17	16
South-East Asia	38	39	34	58	50	49
Western Asia	2.8	2.3	2.3	6.8	4.9	5.3
World	233	244	225	985	927	781

Source: WHO (2010b)

In 2009, Africa was the hardest hit region accounting for 78% of global malaria cases and 91% of global malaria deaths. SSA accounts for 68% of all new adult malaria infections and 91% in children (World Bank, 2011). Global malaria cases peaked at 244 million in 2005, and Africa's malaria cases peaked at 188 million that same year. African malaria deaths showed a monotonic decline from 2000 to 2009 as did global deaths. It is estimated that malaria costs Africa $12 billion per year in lost GDP (World Bank, 2011).The second largest burdens fell upon South-East Asia where malaria cases peaked at 39 million in 2005, and malaria deaths peaked at 58 thousand in 2000. While global and African malaria deaths declined monotonically from 2000 to 2009, South-East Asia's showed falling and rising periods over the decade (for example, deaths dropped to 48 thousand in 2007 and then rose in 2008 and in 2009).

Eleven African countries showed more than 50% reductions in malaria cases over the past decade: Algeria, Botswana, Cape Verde, Eritrea, Madagascar, Namibia, Rwanda, Sao Tome and Principe, South Africa, Swaziland, and Zambia. All of these countries had intense malaria control interventions (World Bank, 2011).

Other Major Diseases

Tuberculosis

Tuberculosis (TB) is an airborne contagious disease which infects one-third of the world's population (WHO, 2010b). Only 5-10% of those infected with TB will become sick or infectious at some time during their lifetime unless they also become infected with HIV/AIDS. HIV, by weakening the immune system, increases the likelihood that a TB-infected person will become sick. Accounting for 13% of AIDS deaths globally, TB is a leading cause of death for HIV-infected individuals. Africa had the most cases of HIV positive TB cases in 2007 (79%) with South Africa accounting for 31% of the African cases (WHO, 2009b).

In 2008, of all developing regions, SSA had the largest incidence of TB cases at 490 per 100,000. HIV is the major factor leading to an increased incidence of TB in Africa since the mid 1990's. The TB mortality figures in Table 13 show SSA had the highest TB mortality rate –52 per 100 thousand in 2008. Thirteen of the 15 countries with the highest TB incidence are in SSA (WHO, 2009b). Contrary to trends elsewhere in the world, SSA shows higher TB incidence and TB deaths rates in 2008 than in 1990. The figures in Table 13 do not include HIV-related TB mortality. TB is second only to HIV in total deaths. Of 1.8 million people dying from TB in 2008, half also had HIV (UN, 2010).

Table 13: Tuberculosis (TB) Incidence and TB Mortality Rates

Region	TB Incidence		TB Deaths	
	1990	**2008**	**1990**	**2008**
SSA	**300**	**490**	**33**	**52**
South-East Asia	440	290	56	37
South Asia	380	220	45	28
Oceania	430	110	50	17
CIS	200	100	26	18
East Asia	270	90	31	12
Latin America & Caribbean	150	40	17	5
West Asia	83	40	9	5
North Africa	80	27	11	4

Source: UN (2010)

Measles and Other Diseases

The story regarding measles in Africa is much happier one than for many other health issues. As a result of the 2001 Measles Initiative, a long-term program to vaccinate 200 million children over five years, measles deaths in Africa decreased by 46% between 1999 and 2003. An additional benefit of the measles vaccination program is that hospital beds are freed up for children suffering from other diseases (UN Foundation News Release).

Porter (2002) notes the problems of accessing health care when the individuals live on off-road locations. Health facilities are rare in such rural settings. Vaccination programs tend to miss these populations. The travel cost to receive medical care is a barrier to the receipt of needed treatment.

For each illness, SSA has the lowest vaccination rate of all regions of the world. No SSA vaccination rate exceeds 90%, and two are below 80%.

Table 14: The Median Percent of Infants (1-Year Olds) Immunized Against Selected Diseases, 2008

Countries and Benchmark	Tuberculosis	Diphtheria, Pertussis, tetanus	Polio	Measles	Hepatitis B
SSA	89	81	79	77	82
Arab States	98	94	97	92	93
Central & Eastern Asia	98	96	96	97	97
Central Asia	97	95	95	97	91
East Asia & Pacific	96	92	92	93	92
Latin America & Caribbean	98	93	93	95	93
South &Western Asia	98	95	95	89	95

Source: UNESCO (2011a)

REFERENCES

Hoffmann, V. 2009. Intrahousehold allocation of free and purchased mosquito nets. *American Economic Review, Papers and Proceedings*. 99(2), 236-241.

Porter, G. 2002. Living in a walking world: rural mobility and social equity issues in Sub-Saharan Africa. *World Development*. 30(2), 285-300.

Roll Back Malaria &World Health Organization (RBM/WHO). 2003. The Abuja Declaration and plan of action.

Roll Back Malaria, World Health Organization and United Nations Childrens' Fund (RBM/WHO/UNICEF). 2005. World Malaria Report.

Roll Back Malaria Partnership. (RBMP). 2008. The global malaria action plan-for a malaria–free world.

UNAIDS. 2008. 2008 Report on the global AIDS epidemic. Geneva, Switzerland.

UNAIDS. 2009a. Annual Report 2009: Uniting the World Against Aids.

UNAIDS. 2009b. AIDS Epidemic Update

UNAIDS. 2010. Report on the Global AIDS Epidemic, 2010.

UNESCO. 2011. "The Hidden Crisis: Armed Conflict and Education." Education for All Global Monitoring Report, 2011. Paris, France.

UNICEF. 2010. Levels and Trends in Child Mortality. Report 2010. New York, NY.

United Nations Foundation. 2005. Measles deaths in Africa dropped by nearly half over five years. New York, NY.

United Nations General Assembly (UNGA). 2001. Declaration on Commitment on HIV/AIDS.
New York, NY.

United Nations General Assembly (UNGA). 2005a. UN 2005 World Summit Outcome. New York, NY.

United Nations General Assembly (UNGA). 2005b. Progress made in the implementation of the Declaration of commitment on HIV/AIDS. New York, NY.

United Nations General Assembly (UNGA). 2010. Keeping the Promise: United To Achieve The Millennium Development Goals. (the 2010 UN Summit) New York, NY.

World Bank. 2003. World Development Report 2004. Washington, DC

World Bank. 2005. Rolling Back Malaria: Global Strategy and Booster Program. Washington, DC

World Bank. 2008. Global Monitoring Report 2008. Washington, DC

World Bank. 2011. Millennium Development Goals, Goal 6. Combat HIV/AIDS, Malaria and Other Diseases by 2015. Washington, DC

World Health Organization. (WHO). 2005a. World Health Report, 2005. Geneva, Switzerland.

World Health Organization (WHO). 2005b. The "3 by 5 Initiative" Progress Report, 2004, (released January 26, 2005). Geneva, Switzerland.

World Health Organization (WHO). 2008. World Malaria Report 2008. Geneva, Switzerland.

World Health Organization (WHO). 2009a. Malaria, Fact Sheet 94. January 2009. Geneva, Switzerland.

World Health Organization (WHO). 2009b. Global Tuberculosis Control. Geneva, Switzerland.

World Health Organization (WHO). 2010a. Trends in Maternal Mortality: 1990-2008. Geneva, Switzerland.

World Health Organization (WHO). 2010b. World Malaria Report 2010: 1990-2008. Geneva, Switzerland

World Health Organization (WHO). 2010c. Tuberculosis. Fact Sheet 104, November. Geneva, Switzerland

CHAPTER 12
MILLENNIUM DEVELOPMENT GOAL VII: ENVIRONMENTAL SUSTAINABILITY

MDG 7: Ensure Environmental Sustainability

Target 10: Integrate the Principles of Sustainable Development into Country Policies and Programmes and Reverse the Loss of Environmental Resources

CLIMATE CHANGE

Natural Disasters and Climate Change

Climate change is a particular case of natural hazard-induced disasters. The UN defines a disaster as:

> A serious disruption of the functioning of a community or a society causing wide-spread human, material, economic or environmental losses which exceed the ability of the affected community or society to cope using its own resources (IDMC, 2011).

The criteria for classifying an event as a disaster include at least one of the following (IDMC, 2011):

- Ten or more people reported as being killed
- 100 or more people reported as being affected
- Declaration of a state of emergency
- Call for international assistance

SSA contributes a negligible amount of emissions which affect the climate; hence policies to reduce climate change globally are not relevant to the region. There is concern that local deforestation can alter local rainfall (Chothia, 2011). The impact of climate change has major consequences for the region.

Hunger and possible famine in SSA caught public attention in late 2010 and increasingly during 2011. In December 2010, *The Economist*, in an article concerning climatic problems in the Sahel, claimed "The biggest fear is that climate change will make survival of the people of the Sahel impossible." The Economist quotes Petra Tschakert, a climate-change expert, as claiming that "the main concern is for the increasingly unpredictable and violent rainfall, not the amount." UNICEF states that malnutrition kills 225,000 children annually in five Sahel countries: Burkina Faso, Chad, Mali, Mauritania, and Niger. These countries are in the western and central regions of the Sahel. Concerns by mid-2011 were focused on the crises in the Horn of Africa countries in the Sahel: Djibouti, Eritrea, Ethiopia, Kenya, Somalia and Uganda. The most severe situations were occurring in southern Somalia.

Following the 1985 famine in Ethiopia, the Famine Early Warning Systems Network (FEWS NET) was established. The system began forecasting a famine threat in Somalia in November, 2010. It is important to know the criteria employed in the FEWS NET system to define these situations and the language associated with varying degrees of severity of food insecurity.

In April, 2011, FEWS NET transitioned from the former Food Insecurity Severity Scale to the Integrated Food Security Phase Classification's IPC Acute Food Insecurity Reference Table. The quantitative limits for food insecurity are set out in Table 1.

Table 1: IPC Acute Food Insecurity Reference Table

Phase	CDR Per 10K/day	U_5DR Per 10K/day	Food HHS	Nutrition Wasting %	Nutrition BMI<18.5 %	Food Access Kcal. pppd	Human Water Access L. pppd
Phase I. None	NDC	NDC	NDC	NDC	NDC	NDC	NDC
Phase II. Stressed	0.5	<1.0	0-1	3-10	10-20	2,100 but Unstable	15 but Unstable
Phase III. Crisis	0.5-1	1-2	Moderate 2-3	10-15	20 -40	2,100 via Asset stripping	7.5-15 via Asset stripping
Phase IV. Hum. Emergency	1-2	2-4	Severe 4-6	15-30	>40	<2,100	< 7.5
Phase V. Catastrophe/ Famine	>2	>4	Severe 6	>30	Far >40	Complete Gap	< 4.0

Source: Table constructed from FEWS NET (2011).CDR=crude death rate, U_5 DR=under five crude death rate, BMI=body mass index, pppd= per person per day, HHS=household hunger scale, NDC=not a defining characteristic.

Table 2: Number of People in the Horn of Africa Countries Requiring Humanitarian Assistance (As of June 29, 2011)

Country	Number As of June 29, 2011	Number As of September 8, 2011
Kenya	3.7 million	4.3 million
Ethiopia	4.8 million	4.8 million
Somalia	3.7 million	4.0 million
Djibouti	165,000	165,642

Source: USAID (2011a, b)

Phase V in the above Table invokes the famine condition for the affected region. The UN declared famine in the Lower Shabelle Region and parts of the Bakool Region on July 20, 2011. During the fall some areas were downgraded from Famine to Humanitarian Emergency (that is from Phase V to Phase IV in the FEWS NET IPC Reference Table).

Terminology is extremely important and sensitive. Famine, while determined in a quantitative assessment, is a very emotive word and hence international organizations are cautious in invoking the term. Governments are reluctant to use the famine word. *The Economist* (2011) noted that "Ethiopia's government will never admit there is famine in the country: to do so would be to say it had failed since 1985." The Somali rebel group, al-Shabab, "claimed the declaration of famine was a western ploy to gain influence" (*The Economist*, 2011). Al-Shabab blamed the crisis on a draught caused by Allah, and people should pray for rain (Chothia, 2011).

The most severe situations have occurred in areas under the control of al-Shabab- a fact noticed by the people who are asking why it has been limited to these areas. The major food shortage in Somalia has resulted in tensions internal to the al-Shabab organization. Some want food aid to be allowed into Somalia while the hard-liners do not (Chothia, 2011). Bans were imposed in 2010 on the World Food Program assistance and that of other humanitarian agencies.

It has been argued that drought is a major contributor to the famine situation but not the only factor. Politics, economics and civil conflict/war also have impacts which exacerbate the severity of the crises. The situation in Somalia is worse than otherwise due to the absence of a functioning central government that could have been a force in dealing with the drought situation. Lack of rain affected local crops and caused prices to increase, making food harder to obtain even when physically available. The banning of food aid, which could have augmented supplies and kept prices down, reinforced the shortages. Al-Shabab expects to be paid by the humanitarian groups for allowing their food to be distributed (through al-Shabab feeding centers). Al-Shabab is accused of stealing food aid to feed itself when it was flowing into the country. The US withheld food aid because it refused to deal with al-Shabab which they have declared as a terrorist organization.

Natural Disasters and Displaced Persons

Natural disasters are a major cause of internal displacement along with conflict, infrastructure projects and human rights violations (IDMC, 2011). Although displaced persons may leave the country or remain within their own country, the large majority of disaster-induced DPs are IDPs. In 2010, 4 million people were displaced due to natural disasters.

Climate-Related Disasters and Displaced Persons

In 2010, 38.3 million people were displaced due to climate- related disasters. The food crisis resulted in an increase in displaced persons for Somalia. The numbers of Somali refugees for 2011 are given in Table 3.

Table 3: Number of Somali Refugees

Country	As of August 3 2011	As of (date)
Kenya	476,808	520,379 (Nov. 14, 2011)
Ethiopia	157,923	181,411 (Nov. 16, 2011)
Djibouti	16,157	18,748 (Oct. 31, 2011)

Source: USAID (2011a, b)

The large refugee camp in Dadaab Kenya is extremely stressed with 380,000 people in a facility designed for a quarter of that number. Refugees complained that there was little difference between the refugee camp and Somalia (Loewenberg, 2011). There are about 70,000 people living outside of the Dadaab camp. The intent is to relocate some of the latter refugees to the Ifo extension which will hold 90,000 refugees when it is fully operational (USAID, 2011b).

While we have been talking about "refugees" caused by natural disasters, these refugees have no legal standing, or protection, under the 1951 Convention. The UNHCR has been assisting but for humanitarian reasons.

TWO ADDITIONAL ENVIRONMENTAL ISSUES

Water Quality

Target 11: Halve By 2015, the Proportion of the Population without Sustainable Access to Safe Drinking Water and Basic Sanitation

Table 4: Proportion of Population Using an Improved Water Source

Region	SSA	Southern Asia	Oceania	North Africa	Western Asia	Eastern Asia	Southeast Asia	Latin America & Caribbean	CIS
1990	49	75	51	86	86	69	72	85	92
2008	60	87	50	92*	90	89*	86*	93*	94

Source: UN (2010). *2015 target met

Four regions have met their 2015 targets. SSA has improved but is still well below its target. Only Oceana has a smaller proportion of population using improved water sources than does SSA.

Table 5: Proportion of Population Using an Improved Water Source, Rural and Urban Areas, 2008

Region	SSA	Southern Asia	Oceania	North Africa	Western Asia	Eastern Asia	Southeast Asia	Latin America & Caribbean	CIS
Rural	47	83	37	87	78	82	81	80	87
Urban	83	95	92	95	96	98	92	97	98

Source: UN (2010)

In all regions the rural community has a smaller proportion of population using improved water sources than does their urban population. SSA and Oceania have the largest urban-rural gaps in access to improved water sources.

Table 6: Proportion of Population Using an Improved Sanitation Facility in Rural and Urban Areas, 2008

Region	SSA	Southern Asia	Oceania	North Africa	Western Asia	Eastern Asia	Southeast Asia	Latin America & Caribbean	CIS
Rural	24	26	45	83	67	53	60	55	83
Urban	44	57	81	94	94	61	79	86	93

Source: UN (2010)

The same pattern holds for rural versus urban users of improved sanitation facilities. In this case SSA's figures are the lowest followed by Oceana's.

Urban Slums

Target 12: By 2020, to have achieved a significant improvement in the lives of at least 100 million slum dwellers.

The proportion of urban populations living in slums in developing countries has declined from 46 percent in 1990 to 33 percent in 2010, while the actual number of people living in slums in developing countries rose from 657 million in 1990 to 828 million in 2010 (UN, 2010).

Table 7: Proportion of Urban Population Living in Slums, 1990, 2000, and 2010

Region	**SSA**	**Southern Asia**	**Oceania**	**North Africa**	**West Asia**	**East Asia**	**Southeast Asia**	**Latin America & Caribbean**	**Developing Regions**
1990	70.0	57.2	24.1	34.4	22.5	43.7	49.5	33.7	46.1
2000	65.0	45.8	24.1	20.3	20.6	37.4	39.6	29.2	39.3
2010	61.7	35.0	24.1	13.3	24.6	28.2	31.0	23.5	32.7

Source: UN (2010)

SSA has the highest proportion of slum livers in urban areas. Note that the target does not specify a baseline from which to judge performance, but rather an actual numerical target is set. The target date is 2020 instead of 2015, and the target is very vague. The UN (2010) believes that the target needs to be redefined.

REFERENCES

Chothia, F. 2011. Could Somali famine deal a fatal blow to al-Shabab? BBC NEWS. August 9. www.bbc.co.uk/news/world-africa

The Economist. 2010. Survival in the Sahel: it's getting harder all the time. December 4th. P 62

The Economist. 2011. The Horn of Africa: Chronicle of a famine foretold. July 30th. P 46

FEWS NET. 2011. Food Security Scale. www.fews.net/ml/en/info/pages/scale.aspx

Internal Displacement Monitoring Center (IDMC). 2011. Displacement due to natural hazard-induced disasters. Norwegian Refugee Council. June.

Loewenberg, S. 2011. Haven and Hell. TIME. August 8, 34-41

USAID. 2011a. Fact Sheet #5. Horn of Africa- Drought. August 4

USAID. 2011b. Fact Sheet #7. Horn of Africa- Drought. November 18

United Nations. 2010. The Millennium Development Goals Report. New York, NY.

CHAPTER 13
THE RESPONSIBILITY TO PROTECT

All that is necessary for the triumph of evil is for good men to do nothing.

(attributed to Edmund Burke).

To observe evil acts and do nothing to stop them is to share responsibility for such acts.

--Tsunesaburo Makiguchi

GOVERNANCE, SOVEREIGNTY AND STATE FAILURE

Failed Governance

UNGA (2005, 2010) emphasized the importance of "good governance and the rule of law" saying they "are essential for sustained, inclusive and equitable economic growth, sustainable development and the eradication of poverty and hunger." UNGA (2005, 2010) also noted particular challenges facing several specific categories of countries.

A particular area needing attention is for improved physical and social infrastructure. Such issues are discussed in UNDP (2003). One of the reasons for China's rapid improvement is the development of infrastructure. Poor infrastructure was one of the reasons given for the poor performance of the Russian economy. Comments by American investors illustrate the broader problems. In their view, the Russian oil industry (in the early 1990s) was fraught with poor infrastructure from the extraction process to the final delivery of product. To deliver product requires decent roads, or pipelines!

Improving infrastructure requires investment which means diverting resources from other uses. This is difficult when incomes are low. This increases the importance of foreign assistance.

Sovereignty and Fixing Failing and Failed States

Ghani and Lockhart (2008) discuss the problem of fixing failed states. While they refer to failed states, in our categories the discussion applies to states characterized as failing (recall from Chapter 5 that only Somalia was ranked as having completely failed, or collapsed, in the statistical rankings). Ghani and Lockhart (2008) argue that a sovereignty gap exists. The gap is the difference between *de jure* sovereignty and *de facto* sovereignty. *De jure* sovereignty refers to the sovereignty ideal. *De facto* sovereignty refers to 'the way things are operating in the real world' where collapsed states do not have the capability to provide basic services for their populations. The authors suggest developing a "sovereignty index," using 10 functions which effective governments should deliver for their populations, to assess the situation. Their approach seems to travel the same ground as those studying governance or state failure, and their approach offers little value-added.

THE RESPONSIBILITY TO PROTECT

The concept of the Responsibility to Protect (known as R2P) is much younger than the state sovereignty concept—by about 300 years! The genesis of R2P occurred mainly in the 1990s and the building blocks include the ideas of key thinkers seeking alternatives to conventional state sovereignty. These include (Evans, 2008):

- Bernard Kouchner and his concept of "Le doit d'ingerence" (the right to intervene)
- the Blair doctrine of "international community"
- the UNDP team headed by Mahbub ul Haq and the "human security" concept
- Francis Deng and the notion of "sovereignty as responsibility"
- Kofi Annan and his "two concepts of sovereignty": state sovereignty and individual sovereignty

Following the UN's Millennium General Assembly in 2000, the Canadian government appointed a special commission, the International Commission on Intervention and State Sovereignty (ICISS), with a charge to find common ground in the debate concerning state sovereignty and humanitarian intervention. The Commission was co-chaired by Gareth Evans, a former Australian foreign minister, and Mohamed Sahnoun, an Algerian diplomat and veteran UN Africa advisor. The Commission published its report 15 months after commencing. The ICISS report contains two basic principles:

a. State sovereignty implies responsibility, and the primary responsibility for the protection of its people lies with the state itself.

b. Where a population is suffering serious harm as a result of internal war, insurgency, repression or state failure, and the state in question is unwilling or unable to halt or avert it, the principle of nonintervention yields to the international responsibility to protect.

R2P also "embraces" three responsibilities: to prevent, to react, and to rebuild. The primary priority of R2P is to "prevent harm" associated with internal conflicts, etc. (Evans, 2008).

The African Union was the first body to endorse the R2P principles. UN Secretary General Kofi Annan, signaled his own support for R2P in his March 2005 report. Later, in September, the concept was endorsed by the 2005 World Summit and was included in its own section: Responsibility to Protect Populations from Genocide, War Crimes, Ethnic Cleansing and Crimes against Humanity, and embodied in paragraphs 138-140. Paragraph 138 of the Report reaffirms the UN's position that sovereign states are responsible for protecting their people from the above crimes. Paragraph 80 reaffirms that the UN Security council has "primary responsibility in the maintenance of international peace and security." Paragraph 139 then notes that in the event a State is unable, or is unwilling, to protect their people, the international community through the UN would be willing to undertake collective action. The General Assembly adopted the Summit Outcome in resolution 60/1(UNGA, 2005). The Security Council reaffirmed the R2P principle in Resolution 1674 (UNSC, 2006). UNGA (2009) is the document for "implementing the responsibility to protect."

The UN Secretary-General (UNGA, 2009) set out a "three- pillar strategy" that flows from Articles 138 and 139 of the 2005 World Summit Outcome:

1) Pillar one-The protection responsibilities of the State
2) Pillar two-International assistance and capacity-building
3) Pillar three-Timely and decisive response

Paragraph 19 stipulates that "National authorities should do their best to assist The International Criminal Court and other international tribunals in locating and apprehending individuals, at whatever level, who are accused of committing or inciting crimes and violations relating to the responsibility to protect" (UNGA, 2009).

Life for R2P has been less easy than its birth and its early years. Bellamy (2010) documents the trials and tribulations of moving the R2P agenda forward. Bellamy lays out some of the countries and/or the organizations that inhibited progress on responding to the protection of the Darfuris in Sudan following a report that the government of Sudan was failing its responsibility to protect the Darfuri (the Arab Group, the Asia Group, and the Organization of the Islamic Conference).

Feinstein and Slaughter (2004) proposed a corollary to R2P, "the Duty to Prevent" regimes from acquiring weapons of mass destruction (WMD). The Duty to Protect provides a rationale for pre-emptive strikes rather than reacting to events that have already occurred. This corollary shows the stress placed on feared rogue states supplying terrorists following the September 11, 2001 attacks.

LACK OF A CREDIBLE THREAT TO INTERVENE AND/OR PROSECUTE

Cry 'Havoc', and let slip the dogs of war.[1]
--Mark Anthony in *Julius Caesar*, Shakespeare, 1601

Do not cry havoc, where you should but hunt with modest warrant.[2]
--*Coriolanus*, Shakespeare, 1607.

Above we argued that the perpetrators of the horrendous violations discussed in this paper do so because they gain personal or group benefits. Given their self-interest in their acts, the mere passing of a law to cease such behavior is not likely to achieve any results in the absence of a credible threat of adverse consequences to the perpetrators. To the extent that the international community is reluctant to face down the perpetrators with police/military force if necessary nothing will change. The perpetrators are like the school yard bully who goes unchallenged and keep on bullying. As supporters of R2P argue intervention with force should be the last resort, but it should be clear that the option is serious if all else fails. For those who object at all, look for their special interests.

UN PEACEKEEPING MISSIONS

UN Peacekeeping missions are like a halfway house in the threat continuum. In fact, former Secretary-General Dag Hammarskjold characterized peacekeeping as belonging to "Chapter VI and a half," between peaceful dispute resolution of Chapter VI and the more forceful action permitted under Chapter VII.

The UN began peacekeeping missions in 1948 as a result of conflict in the Middle East. The military, arriving in June 1948, were unarmed. The first armed contingent was established following the 1956 war to provide a buffer between Israeli and Egyptian forces.

As of September 30, 2011 there have been 66 missions. Fifty-one missions are completed, and 15 are currently in operation. Twenty-one (41%) of the completed missions were in SSA, and these are listed with their respective time periods in Table 1.

Table 1: UN Peacekeeping Missions Completed in SSA

Country/Region	Time Period of Mission
Congo	July 1960-June 1964
Congo	Nov. 1999-July 2010
Angola	Dec. 1988-May 1991
Aouzou Strip	May-June 1994
Namibia	April 1989-March 1990
Angola	May 1991-Feb. 1995
Somalia	April 1992-March 1993
Mozambique	Dec.1992-Dec. 1994
Cote d'Ivoire	May 2003-April 2004
Somalia	March 1993-March 1995
Rwanda/Uganda	June 1993-Sept.1994
Liberia	Sept.1993-Sept.1997
Rwanda	Oct.1993-March 1996
Angola	Feb. 1995-June 1997
Angola	June 1997-Feb.1999
Sierra Leone	July 1998-Oct. 1999
Sierra Leone	Oct.1999-Dec. 2005
CAR	April 1998-Feb. 2000
CAR and Chad	Sept.2007-Dec.2010
Burundi	June 2004-Dec. 2006
Ethiopia/Eritrea	Sept. 2000-July 2008

Source: Infoplease.com (2011)

Of the 15 active operations, five are in SSA, and one is in North Africa. The six African countries are listed in Table 2.

Table 2: Personnel Involved in Current Peacekeeping Operations in Africa and Totals for All Current Missions (As of September 30, 2011)

Country/Region	Starting Date	Uniformed Personnel	Civilian Personnel	UN Volunteers	Fatalities
Western Sahara	April 1991	230	264	18	15
DR Congo	June 2010	18,914	3,800	591	31
Cote d'Ivoire	April 2004	10,648	814	253	82
Liberia	Sept.2003	9,216	1,476	240	161
South Sudan	July 2011	5,303	623+	206	1
Darfur	July 2007	23,162	4046	477	95
Total of 15 Current Missions	------	97,675	19,628	2,267	2,941

Source: UN Peacekeeping (2011)

In total, about 120,000 UN personnel were involved in peacekeeping missions as of September, 30 2011. The largest allocation, about 28,000 people, is for Darfur. The largest number of fatalities (161) occurred in Liberia. The second largest number of fatalities (95) occurred in Darfur.

UN Peacekeeping Critics

Despite the humanitarian reasons for peacekeeping missions, they do have their detractors. Pattison (2010) provides a brief overview of the different criticisms.

One objection concerns the lack of a UN standing army. This puts the UN in the position of needing to amass a force using personnel volunteered by its members. The deployment system is laborious and time consuming. Troops arrive without appropriate equipment. Due to the multi-national makeup of the troops, integration is difficult. Corruption within the UN force has been a problem on occasion.

Who Should Intervene?

If intervention is warranted, the next issue question is: "who should intervene?" Pattison (2010) tackles this important question. He specifies the following two questions that need to be addressed:

1. Who has the right to intervene?
2. Who has the duty to intervene?

To have the right to intervene, interveners need to possess an adequate degree of legitimacy. That is, they need to possess a likelihood of being successful. They also need to be engaged in humanitarian intervention. To have the duty to intervene, interveners need to satisfy the first question and be the most legitimate (generally the most effective) agent.

Pattison (2010) advocates that intervention "be undertaken by a hybrid solution or NATO. If these agents fail to act, [then] the responsibility to protect then falls on states, coalitions of the willing, the UN, and regional organizations (and PMCs [private military companies]) in descending order."

ENDNOTES

1. Havoc was a military order for the soldiers to begin pillage and chaos. The dogs of war are the soldiers.
2. This quote is strikingly similar in intent with the modern day concept of using the minimum force to achieve an objective.

REFERENCES

Bellamy, A. 2010. The Responsibility to Protect --Five Years On. International Coalition for the Responsibility to Protect.

Evans, G. 2008. *The Responsibility to Protect.* The Brookings Institution.

Feinstein, L., and Slaughter, A-M. A Duty to Prevent. *Foreign Affairs.* 83(1), 136-150. 2004.

Ghani, A. and Lockhart, C. 2008. *Fixing Failed States.* Oxford University Press. New York, NY.

Infoplease.com. 2011. UN Peacekeeping Missions. www.infoplease.com . Retrieved 11-8-2011.

Pattison, J. 2010. *Humanitarian Intervention & the Responsibility to Protect: Who Should Intervene?* Oxford University Press. New York, NY.

UN General Assembly (UNGA). 2005. 2005 World Summit Outcome.

UN General Assembly (UNGA). 2009. Implementing the responsibility to protect: Report of the Secretary-General.

UN Peacekeeping. 2011. Peacekeeping Fact Sheet: 9-30-2011.

UN Security Council (UNSC). 2006. Wide-Ranging Text on Civilians in Armed Conflict Strongly Condemns Targeting of Civilians, Sexual Violence, Abuse by Peacekeepers. Resolution 1674.

CHAPTER 14
SOME FINAL OBSERVATIONS

The first part of this chapter is an addendum dealing with armed conflicts occurring, or continuing, after the main chapters were completed. The second section provides brief insights to some topics of an international nature which involve, or impact, Sub-Saharan Africa. These are topics for a more detailed treatment in subsequent research.

ARMED CONFLICTS

Sudan

In 2011, Sudan was divided into two countries: Sudan in the north and South Sudan. South Sudan is struggling to survive infancy. It is dealing with assaults from Sudan and from ethnic clashes within South Sudan.

There are reports that Sudan has conducted air raids killing South Sudanese civilians, mainly cattle herders, in the West Bahr al-Ghazal state. South Sudan's Unity state has also been bombed including the Yida refugee camp (BBC, 2011a). There have also been a number of clashes along the Sudan/South Sudan border which has not been officially designated. Jem (the Justice and Equality Movement), the Darfur- based rebel group, has crossed into South Sudan with a force of 350 members to fight Sudan's forces (BBC, 2011a).

Within South Sudan the Lou Nuer tribe has attacked the town of Pibor, home to the Murle tribe. UN forces and the South Sudanese army were unable to hold back the 6,000 fighters from the Lou Nuer tribe. About 20,000 persons fled before an attack on the town of Lukangol which was burned (BBC, 2012a). The clashes are a result of cattle rustling. Cattle are a store of wealth in this poor country. Cattle are used, among other things, to provide dowries for brides.

Nigeria

An Islamist group, Boko Haram (the name means "Western education is forbidden"), has been conducting attacks in Nigeria. This has led Nigerian President Goodluck Jonathan to declare a state of emergency in areas which have been attacked by the group (BBC, 2011b). Parts of Nigeria's borders with Niger, Chad and Cameroon will be closed. Boko Haram has bombed the UN Headquarters and churches as well.

Nigeria is also facing ethnic violence in eastern regions. The ethnic clashes between the Ezza and Ezilo peoples are being caused by a land dispute (BBC, 2012b).

Somalia

As we have discussed above Somalia is a failed state which has not had a strong central government for about 20 years. The fight against al-Shabab, the extreme Islamist group, is changing shape. In October, Kenya attacked the group in Somalia for abduction carried out in Kenya. Kenya's Parliament has approved the Kenyan forces being integrated into the African Union (AU) force engaged in fighting al-Shabab. Ethiopia has agreed to support the AU-Kenyan forces campaign. Djibouti and Sierra Leone have also promised to send troops in support of the AU forces (BBC, 2011c). On the other side, Eritrea has been accused of sending weapons to al-Shabab, an accusation which Eritrea denies (BBC, 2011d).

INTERNATIONAL ACTIVITIES INVOLVING OR IMPACTING, SUB-SAHARAN AFRICA

Human Trafficking

Human trafficking is covered by the Protocol to Prevent, Suppress and Punish Trafficking in Persons, also known as the Trafficking in Persons Protocol (TPP). The TPP, a protocol to the Convention against Transnational Organized Crime, defines Human Trafficking as "the recruitment, transportation, transfer, harboring or receipt of persons by means of threat, or use of force or other forms of coercion, of abduction, of fraud or deception, or the abuse of power or of a position of vulnerability or of the giving or receiving of payments or benefits to achieve the consent of a person having control over another person, for the purpose of exploitation" where exploitation includes " at a minimum, the exploitation of the prostitution of others or other forms of sexual exploitation, forced labor or services, slavery or practices similar to slavery, servitude or the removal of organs" (TPP, 2000). Globally, between 700 thousand and 4 million women, children and men are trafficked annually (IAST).Between 600 thousand and 800 thousand are trafficked across national boundaries. Of the top 11 originating countries only one SSA country is listed: Nigeria. No SSA country is listed in the "high demand" list.

The Child Services Prevention Act (CSPA) of 2008 defines child soldiers as those under age 18 "serving in any capacity including serving in a support role such cooks, porters, messengers, medics, guard or sex slave." Children under 15 years of age recruited voluntarily into government armed forces are also classified as child soldiers under the CSPA. The four SSA countries "listed" by CSPA are: Chad, DR Congo, Somalia, and Sudan.

The US Department of State's Trafficking in Persons Report 2011 lists eight SSA countries in Tier 3 countries which do not comply with the minimum standards and are not making significant efforts to do so. The Tier 3 countries are: Eritrea, Mauritania, Guinea-Bissau, Sudan, CAR, DR Congo, Equatorial Guinea, Zimbabwe, and Madagascar.

Maritime Piracy

Maritime piracy in recent times is a lucrative business and a global security threat. African piracy attacks are conducted predominately by Somali pirates off East Africa. There were 266 pirate attacks globally in the first six months of 2011. Of these attacks, 163 (or, 61%) were conducted by Somali pirates in the Gulf of Aden (News Release, 2011). West Africa is becoming another arena for piracy events with a likely shift occurring from Nigerian waters to those off Benin (News Release, 2011). The cost of global piracy is estimated to be \$7-\$12 billion annually (Ploch et al., 2011). In 2010, there were more than 1,180 hostages taken by pirates for ransom. Eighty-six percent of these were taken by Somali pirates. Ransoms to Somali pirates average about \$5 million per ship (Ploch et al., 2011). The piracy problem in Somalia is attributed to the absence of a functioning government in Somalia. Several years ago, the shipping firms preferred to pay the ransoms rather than risk their ships, people and loads. This overlooked the perverse incentives it gave to the pirates. Essentially, the shipping lines were sending the signal "capture us and we'll give you money." Naturally, insurance rates began to adjust upwards from \$500 per ship, per voyage to \$150,000 per ship, per voyage (Ploch et al., 2011). Countries have become proactive in attempting to stop, or fend off, the attacks. Naval forces from several countries now patrol the waters. The EU, NATO, China and Russia are participating along with US naval forces.

Poaching

Poaching, for the purpose of this section, is defined as "the illegal hunting, killing or capturing of animals" (Magelah, 2011). Many animals are the object of poaching activities. Poaching can substantially lower population sizes of the targeted animals. In severe cases this may lead to extinction of the species. As population levels are lowered species first become Vulnerable, then Threatened, and finally Endangered (or Critically Endangered). AAW (2009) indicated that there were well over 5,000 species of animals and birds classified as Threatened or Endangered. For this brief introduction we select one animal which is receiving a lot of attention lately, the Rhinoceros. Although there are rhinos in Asia we limit ourselves, of course, to Africa.

There are two species of rhinoceros in Africa: the White Rhinoceros, and the Black Rhinoceros. Both species are now extinct in Uganda (Magelah, 2011). We cannot conclude that all of the species in Uganda were hunted to extinction in Uganda. Rhinos like other animals (and humans) can migrate when threatened. So, some living Ugandan rhinos may have left the country in search of safer grounds.

Table 1 shows the time profiles of the population sizes of the rhinos in South African.

Table 1: Population Size Profiles of White and Black Rhinos (2004-2010), and the Number of Rhinos Poached (2000-2011) in South Africa

	2002	2003	2004	2005	2006
White Pop'n	---	---	10,796	13,555	15,941
Black Pop'n	---	---	1,328	1,384	1,456
Number Poached	25	22	10	13	24

Table 1 cont.

	2007	2008	2009	2010	2011
White Pop'n	16,273	18,352	19,409	18,780	---
Black Pop'n	1,512	1,587	1,678	1,916	---
Number Poached	13	83	122	333	382

Source: Developed from two charts in SRP (2011).

The White Rhino has shown steady growth from 2004 to 2009. The increase of 8,613 over this time period is an increase of about 80%. The population shows a drop of 629 in 2010. The 2010 population size is striking when compared to the 1993 size of 6,376!

The Black Rhino population has shown a steady upward trend over the time span shown but from a much lower size. The growth from 1,384 in 2004 to 1,916 in 2010 amounts to a 44% increase.

In the six years ranging from 2002-2007, the number of rhinos poached never exceeded 25. In 2008, rhino poaching levels jumped up tremendously to more than three times the highest level in the preceding six years. The 2011 figure is the count to November 26, 2011, and the poaching number is expected to top 400 for the year. The reason for the upward jump in poaching is the increased demand for the rhino horn in Asia, especially in China. The rhino horn is sought for its medicinal value. South Africa is where most of the poaching is occurring (Conniff, 2011). The African Conservancy says price of rhino horns up to $40,000 per kilo have been recorded.

After this section was initially drafted, a report released by an international wildlife trade group Traffic indicated that 2011 saw more elephant tusks seized than in any other year since 1989 when ivory trade was banned. The seizure amounted to 23 tons of ivory which translates to, at least, 2,500 dead animals. Like the rhino horns, the major demand comes from Asia, especially from China and Thailand. Unlike the rhino horn, the elephant tusk is sought for its decorative opportunities. South Africa, Botswana, Namibia and Zimbabwe willingly sell their stockpiles of ivory (BBC, 2011e).

THE FINAL COMMENT

Our book ends here and now. However, the story about Africa continues, and "there is always something new coming out of Africa."

REFERENCES

African Conservancy. Wildlife and Conservation Statistics. www.africanconservancy.org/about/documents/facts.pdf

BBC NEWS. 2011a. Southerners 'killed by Sudan air raids'. 12-29-2011. www.bbc.co.uk/news.

BBC NEWS. 2011b. Boko Haram attacks prompt Nigerian state of emergency. 11-31-2011. www.bbc.co.uk/news.

BBC NEWS. 2011c. Kenya troops to 'join Somalia's African Union force'. 12-07-2011. www.bbc.co.uk/news.

BBC NEWS. 2011d. Eritrea denies sending weapons to al-Shabab in Somalia. 12-29-2011. www.bbc.co.uk/news.

BBC NEWS. 2011e. Elephant poaching: 'record year' for ivory seizures. 12-29-2011. www.bbc.co.uk/news.

BBC NEWS. 2012a. UN warns South Sudanese to flee deadly ethnic vendetta. 1-2-2012. www.bbc.co.uk/news.

BBC NEWS. 2012b. At least 50 killed in ethnic clashes in eastern Nigeria. 1-1-2012. www.bbc.co.uk/news.

Conniff, R. 2011. Defending the Rhino. *Smithsonian*, November 2011, 64-72.

Magelah, P. 2011. Poaching. Encyclopedia of Earth. www.eoearth.org/article/Poaching

News Release. 2011. Maritime agency sounds West Africa piracy alarm. 9-14-2011. Mg.co.za/printformat/single/2011-09-14-west-africa-becomes-ship-hijacking-hotspot/

Ploch, L. et al. 2011. Piracy off the Horn of Africa. Congressional Research Service (CRS).

Stop Rhino Poaching (SRP). 2011. Rhino Poaching Statistics. www.stoprhinopoaching.com/statistics.aspx

United Nations General Assembly (UNGA). 2000. United Nations Convention against Transnational Organized Crime.

United Nations General Assembly (UNGA). 2000. Protocol to Prevent, Suppress and Punish Trafficking in Persons (the Trafficking in Persons Protocol, TPP).

United States Department of State (State Department). (2011). Trafficking in Persons Report, June 2011.

www.ingramcontent.com/pod-product-compliance
Lightning Source LLC
LaVergne TN
LVHW020412220926
848484LV00016B/2552/J
* 9 7 8 0 9 8 5 3 9 4 9 0 5 *